D1068525

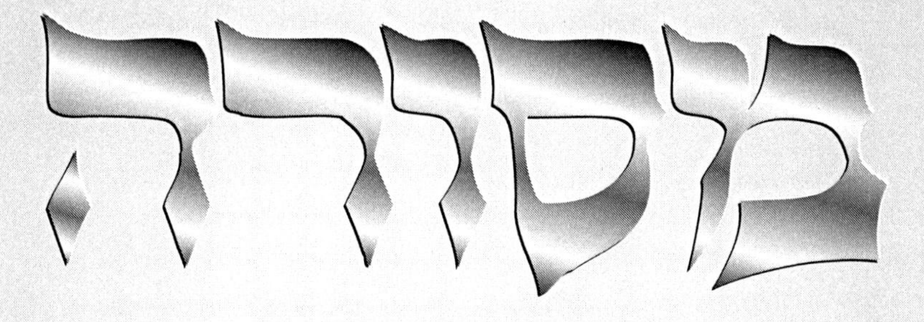

ArtScroll® Series

Rabbi Nosson Scherman / Rabbi Gedaliah Zlotowitz
General Editors
Rabbi Meir Zlotowitz ז״ל, *Founder*

Captivating stories rich with meaning

Published by

RABBI YECHIEL SPERO

FIRST EDITION
First Impression ... March 2022

Published and Distributed by
MESORAH PUBLICATIONS, LTD.
313 Regina Avenue / Rahway, N.J 07065

Distributed in Europe by
LEHMANNS
Unit E, Viking Business Park
Rolling Mill Road
Jarow, Tyne & Wear, NE32 3DP
England

Distributed in Australia and New Zealand by **GOLDS WORLDS OF JUDAICA**
3-13 William Street
Balaclava, Melbourne 3183
Victoria, Australia

Distributed in Israel by
SIFRIATI / A. GITLER — BOOKS
POB 2351
Bnei Brak 51122

Distributed in South Africa by
KOLLEL BOOKSHOP
Northfield Centre, 17 Northfield Avenue
Glenhazel 2192, Johannesburg, South Africa

ARTSCROLL® SERIES
WHAT A STORY!

To contact the author with comments or stories,
he can be reached via e-mail at chiely1@gmail.com

ITEM CODE: WHATH
ISBN 10: 1-4226-3115-X / ISBN 13: 978-1-4226-3115-7

Typography by CompuScribe at ArtScroll Studios, Ltd.
Bound by Sefercraft, Quality Bookbinders, Ltd., Rahway N.J. 07065

מכתב ברכה מאת הרב דוד קוויאט זצ״ל
ר״מ בישיבת מיר
ורב דאגודת ישראל סניף חפץ חיים

ב״ה

י״ג מנחם אב תשס״ג

מכתב ברכה

לכבוד ידידי הרב יחיאל ספירא שליט״א, רבי בישיבת הק׳ חפץ חיים בבלטימור,

הנה בא לפני עלים מספרך אשר כתבת ושמו ״נתרגש פון א מעשה״ הנה כשמו כן הוא כולו ספורים יקרים המביא רגשות קודש להקוראים בו, מה שנחוץ זה למאוד לחזק האמונה וללמוד איך להתנהג באמונה ובמדות טובות כמו שעולה מהספורים. ולכן אברכהו שיצליח בספרו ושיהנו הקוראים בו,והשם יתב׳ יברכהו להרבות תורה ומוסר ויגדיל תורה ויאדיר.

ממני ידידו המברכו בכל לב

דוד קוויאט

דוד קוויאט

Michtav Berachah written for *Touched by a Story*

Acknowledgments

EIN ANACHNU MASPIKIM LE'HODOS LECHA HASHEM Elokeinu!

And for His many messengers...

More than 20 years ago, I received a phone call from **Reb Nosson Scherman**. I remember where I was and what I was doing when he delivered the news that ArtScroll was accepting my manuscript. It was mostly chicken scratch. Unedited chicken scratch. 10 stories in all. When I expressed hesitation that I had only submitted 10 stories, he assured me, "We believe in you." Four of the most meaningful words I've ever heard.

Reb Meir Zlotowitz continues to be the *meilitz yosher* for all of ArtScroll's transformative global impact.

Reb Gedaliah Zlotowitz has taken ArtScroll to new, unimaginable heights. That in itself is truly remarkable. But doing so with the smile and warmth that long ago became his trademark makes the transition even more extraordinary. As a close friend, I feel fortunate to watch him work his magic from a box-seat view. Best seat in the house.

Reb Sheah Brander's elegant handprint is found on every eye-pleasing page of ArtScroll's every book.

Reb Avrohom Biderman's friendship extends well beyond the books I write. When others ask for guidance in the world of writing and publishing, Avrohom is the go-to person. He gives of his valuable time and is ready to help. Many authors owe their success to his advice. I am no exception.

I have now had the privilege of working with **Reb Ahron Zlotowitz** on several projects. He's a real talent. Humble and eager are a great combination. *Ve'hachut hameshulash lo bimheirah yinateik*. Ahron is a rising star, and for very good reason.

My gratitude also extends to **Reb Yitzchok Hisiger**, my *chaver* from his years at the Yated, who has added so much to ArtScroll in such a short amount of time.

Reb Mendy Herzberg would do well in the circus, juggling countless responsibilities with a smile and grace.

Reb Eli Kroen deserves more credit for this cover than ever before. His bold and fearless creativity allowed the cover to pop off the page and grab the consumer's attention. Eli: "What a Cover!"

Mrs. Mindy Stern always possesses the right words. Her exceptional editing enhances just about every book I write. Thanks, as well, to **Mrs. Toby Goldzweig** for inserting corrections and changes, and to **Mrs. Faygie Weinbaum** for her meticulous proofreading. And as always, **Mrs. Estie Dicker** did an expert job in paginating, polishing each book she touches until it sparkles.

It is now 15 years that **Mrs. Tova Salb** has been editing my books, articles, and more. Not only is she an excellent literary and content editor, but she has an innate sense of what works and what doesn't. I am eternally indebted for her availability, effort, and expertise.

I would also like to express my gratitude to the *mosdos* that have invited me to speak at their events over the years. As well, thank you to the many individuals who tell me their stories, a number of which appear in this book. Though I am not able to use every story, I am appreciative nonetheless; I may make use of them in a future volume. Please note: In order to protect the privacy of the protagonists, I have often taken the liberty of hiding the identity of the people in a story.

An added note of special thanks to a dear friend who wishes to remain anonymous but is always someone I can count on. May his efforts be a *zechus* for the *aliyah* of the *neshamos* of his father and father-in-law.

Additionally, a group of family friends, "Besties of '89," were instrumental and supportive in choosing the name of this book. Truth is, they are always there, and we are very thankful.

My parents, **Dr.** and **Mrs. Abba Spero**, and my in-laws, **Rabbi** and **Mrs. Yehuda Lefkovitz**, are there for our family in every which way. We are always grateful for their input and wisdom. May they have *arichus yamim ve'shanim* and may we always be *zocheh* to give them *nachas*.

Tzvi and **Rochel Leah**, **Avromi** and **Leora**, **Efraim** and **Sora Leba**, **Daniel** and **Miri**, **Shmueli**, **Chana Leah**, **Henni**, and **Chayala**: Remember to always live for others.

And finally, to their mother and my wife, **Chumi**. No one does either job better.

May Hashem continue to give us the *siyata d'Shmaya* to serve Him in the best way we can.

Yechiel Spero
Adar I, 5782

To Tell and to Listen

THERE'S LISTENING AND THERE'S LISTENING.

Stories have been a part of our history since the beginning of time. The world begins with *maaseh Bereishis*, the story of Creation. The Jewish people are born as a nation through *sippur Yetzias Mitzrayim,* the story of our Exodus.

Many wonder how it is that there are so many stories. Where do they all come from?

The truth is that as long as the Jewish people exist, there will always be stories. Every time a Yid overcomes adversity, there is a story in the making.

Something special and inspiring. Something worth sharing.

Since it is his personal story, he may choose to keep it to himself. But if he decides to share it with others, it will most likely inspire, helping those in similar situations grow from his experience.

Perhaps that is the allegorical meaning of Hashem's instructions to Avraham (*Bereishis* 15:5), "*U'sefor hakochavim.*" Simply understood, He was telling Avraham to count the stars. But maybe there is more.

The word *u'sefor* (וספר) has the same root as *sippur* (סיפור), story. Hashem may be instructing us to tell our stories, the stories of the Jewish people, who are compared to the stars.

Every Yid glistens and glows. Each one shines.

But though they burn brightly, stars are far off in the distance, millions of miles from us. How much can we really appreciate them?

Could it be, though, that the stories of our stars are closer than we think?

Maybe...

In every story, there is the teller and the listener.

The tellers seek to transmit the story to the best of their ability. If they succeed, then not only will their listeners appreciate the story, but they will be transported; they will feel very much a part of the tale. Almost like another character, watching the story unfold — in real time and real life. The great *maggidim* of yesteryear sought to achieve this, camouflaging their messages of *mussar* in stories and parables, turning their listeners into more than onlookers.

Rav Shalom Schwadron did not always intend to be a *maggid*. But he was once asked to substitute for one of the *maggidim* who gave a weekly *shmuess* in the Zichron Moshe shul, which he did. The next day, he met one of the attendees, who admitted that he was going through a very challenging time, and the stories and messages Rav Shalom had shared the night before had changed his perspective.

And eventually his life.

That feedback changed Rav Shalom's, as well.

Little did he know, he would impact generations.

One story.

But you really need to listen.

When you truly listen to a story, it can make an indelible mark on your *neshamah*.

When Yisro heard the news that the Jewish people had been miraculously saved, he blessed Hashem (*Shemos* 18:10), "*Baruch Hashem...*"

The Imrei Emes asks: How could he have made such a *bera-*

chah? Doesn't the Mishnah (*Berachos* 9:1) state explicitly that one may only recite a blessing on a miracle that happened to Bnei Yisrael if he sees the exact spot of the miracle? Yisro wasn't in Mitzrayim at the time of the miracles, which should have precluded him from reciting the blessing.

The answer, says the Gerrer Rebbe, is that if one really listens to a story, "*achein nimtza sham* — he is indeed there."

Period.

There for the story. There for the lesson. There for the impact. There for the story to do what it is meant to accomplish.

Nothing in this world happens in a vacuum. "*Sham*," there, is our destination. It is the place we are meant to reach.

Dear reader, enjoy the book. I hope the stories entertain you. But if you really listen, then you will hear the messages they are meant to carry.

The stars will shine brightly.

And so will you.

Table of Contents

Tefillah

Chesed

Hashgachah Pratis

Chinuch

Gevurah

Emunah

Teshuvah

Mitzvos

PLANTING A SEED

The Show Must Go On

Rabbanit Massouda Vaknin — the wife of Rav Yitzchak Vaknin, rav of Maalot — was a remarkable woman who stood by her husband's side for over 65 years of marriage. A loving grandmother and great-grandmother, the rabbanit knew the birthdays of over 100 grandchildren and great-grandchildren. Though very educated and accomplished, she never spoke about her own achievements, only giving credit and accolades to others. In addition, she and her husband lost a 9-year-old child when he was hit by a car, yet she did not express any anger or resentment toward the driver who ran a red light and killed her son. She even encouraged him throughout his court case and tried to lift his spirits.

Massouda grew up in Tangier, Morocco. After their marriage, Rav Yitzchak and Rabbanit Massouda made their home in Tangier, where they shared an apartment with another family. Despite the difficulties involved in such an arrangement, they did it with a smile. These early years helped the rabbanit understand the ramifications of poverty. Years later, her warmth and encouragement breathed life into the many downtrodden individuals who frequented her home. In many cases, at first they came knocking on the door for a donation, but by the time they were finished, their visit could turn into a weeks' long stay.

DURING THE EARLY YEARS OF THEIR MARRIAGE, RAV Yitzchak served as *menahel* of a girls' school, and the rabbanit assisted him every step of the way. One day, they received word that one of their students, Mazal, was engaged to a wonderful boy named Chanan, and the entire school celebrated together.

Chanan, an orphan who came from an impoverished family, was not able to arrange a *Shabbat Chatan* (the celebration on the Shabbat after the wedding among Jews of Sephardic descent) for himself and his *kallah*. When she heard this, the rabbanit was distraught. How could a newlywed couple not have a memorable Shabbat to celebrate their union? Immediately, she sent a message that she would take care of all the details of the Shabbat. Despite the fact that she too did not have any money, she was not going to allow such a "minor detail" to stop her from moving forward. She got to work quickly and invited Mazal's family and Chanan's family and all of their children. Next, she secured a room to host the celebration and arranged for sleeping accommodations for the two large families, and then she began shopping and cooking. No expense was spared; she made sure it was a Shabbat to remember.

When Mazal heard what the rabbanit was doing for her and Chanan, she grew emotional at this outpouring of love. Instead of a minimalist Shabbat with a melancholy feel to it, the young couple would enjoy a Shabbat overflowing with joy and happiness. The unexpectedness of it all only added to the *simchah*.

Chanan and Mazal beamed all Shabbat. So moved was Mazal that she accepted upon herself that from then on, any time an orphaned *chatan* was unable to afford a *Shabbat Chatan*, she would cook it herself.

Decades passed. Chanan and Mazal built a large, beautiful family of their own. Mazal kept up with the rabbanit, never forgetting her kindness. When Rabbanit Massouda passed away, Mazal, now an older woman, came to be *menachem avel* and related, "Over the years, I have had the *zechut* to cook tens, if not hundreds, of meals for the *Shabbat Chatan* for poor and orphaned *chatanim* who had nowhere else to turn. Instead of a non-celebratory first Shabbat, they experienced a Shabbat of beauty and *simchah*.

"Imagine," continued Mazal, "the scene when the rabbanit went up to *Shamayim*. She must have been shown all of the magnificent events she had orchestrated. In all likelihood, she looked bewildered. 'I never arranged these. Only once, 67 years ago, did I make a *Shabbat Chatan* for a couple who didn't have any money.'

"At that point, the truth must have been revealed, how that one Shabbat developed into dozens of Shabbatot, saving so many young couples from embarrassment and sadness."

Often, we may hesitate to perform one act of kindness or do one altruistic deed, rationalizing, "I can't keep it up, so why even try?"

In truth, though, if we do our little bit, there is no telling where it may lead.

Doctor of Dedication

DURING THE EARLY YEARS OF WORLD WAR II, THE JEWS were crammed into ghettos and forced to live in subhuman conditions. With ten people to a room and little food, as well as rampant disease, many perished. It was not unusual to walk in the street and see corpses of people who had passed away from starvation. The *chevrah kaddisha* was overwhelmed; their wagons were filled with *meisim*. Those still alive couldn't help but wonder about their fate. Misery filled the air. Although the Germans were only just beginning to butcher the

Jews, these inhumane conditions gave rise to feelings of desperation and hopelessness, desensitizing the Jews, just what the Germans wanted of their prey.

Courageous mothers and fathers did their utmost to provide for their children, but the food was sparse and children often went to bed without eating, crying from hunger — and also from fear. Many sensed that the worst was yet to come. They searched for escape routes and gathered their valuables, hoping to put them to use as bribes to safety, but there were few answers to their predicament.

The clock was ticking.

One day, Leah, a mother of a large family, turned ill. At first, she tried to ignore her pains and aches, hoping the symptoms would disappear on their own. But they would not. As her condition deteriorated, she was astute enough to know that if she remained where she was, she would most certainly die. She desperately needed medical attention. Grabbing the last monies she possessed, she fled the ghetto and ran to Dr. Magda Bukowski, a Polish doctor she was acquainted with.

Furious at Leah for risking her life by leaving the ghetto, Dr. Bukowski wanted to close the door on her. However, after Leah begged for compassion, Dr. Bukowski allowed her entry, then examined her and administered the medication she needed. Leah tried to give her the money she had brought along but the doctor, suddenly more compassionate and understanding, told Leah to hold onto it for future needs.

Dr. Bukowski inquired about the conditions in the ghetto and what life was like there. She had heard some rumors but could never have fathomed how bad things really were. Although she lived only a few blocks away, it was like she was living on the other side of the planet. The Polish people wanted to turn a blind eye and pretend that war crimes were not occurring daily, practically under their noses. It was better for their conscience and emotional well-being this way.

Nevertheless, once she heard directly from Leah about the horrific conditions in the ghetto that made it almost impossible to live as a regular human being, Dr. Bukowski said to her, "In your condition, you cannot return to the ghetto." Leah looked at her incredulously. What was she suggesting?

As if reading Leah's mind, Dr. Bukowski continued, "It will be a very dangerous move, but I have an attic above my house and I'm willing to hide you there." The about-face was startling, but obviously Dr. Bukowski was appalled by what she had heard and really wanted to help.

Leah was very grateful for the offer and would have happily taken her up on it, but there was one "minor" problem. "I have thirteen people directly under my care. My children need me and I will not leave them."

The doctor did not hesitate, her generous disposition widening by the moment. "Then bring all thirteen of them over here, and I'll hide everyone."

It took a few days for everyone to disguise themselves in order to make the short but life-threatening journey to the Bukowski house. But within a few days' time, they were all there. And over the next six years, this remarkable Polish doctor hid all fourteen of them in her attic.

Even more astonishing is the fact that Dr. Bukowski's home was situated opposite Gestapo headquarters. Every day, numerous Gestapo officers, who specialized in finding Jews, walked by her apartment. Other righteous gentiles risked their lives to save the Jews and were caught. An hour after their discovery, they were dangling in the town square for their treasonous behavior. But that thought didn't stop Dr. Bukowski.

Six years after Leah's initial visit to Dr. Bukowski, the Germans were finally defeated and Leah and her thirteen charges left the attic. Malnourished, weak, and traumatized — yet alive. The Al-mighty had sent them a special angel to watch over them. Eventually, they all recovered and reestablished their lives, each building a family.

Years later, Leah, together with multitudes of children, grandchildren, great-grandchildren, and even great-great-grandchildren, gathered for a reunion in America. By that time, there were over 300 family members. One non-family member was also in attendance: the heroine, Dr. Bukowski, the compassionate Polish doctor, joined, as well.

After Rav Shimshon Pincus told this incredible tale, he asked the obvious question. How did this non-Jewish Polish woman reach such an exceptional level of mesirus nefesh, to risk everything to save Leah and her entire family, especially considering that she seemed to be so uncaring in the first place? Moreover, she knew that what she was doing was extremely dangerous, and moreover, she was barely acquainted with Leah! And yet, she saved Leah and all her family and protected them for six years! How did it happen?

Rav Shimshon revealed a fundamental concept in the inner workings of kindness, or for that matter, any noble act or deed. It is true that Dr. Bukowski initially displayed little interest in helping Leah. Yet the moment she opened the door, that action created a shoresh, a root, of a good deed, a maaseh tov, which grew into another kind deed and another. As she took care of Leah without charging her, the root bloomed into a tree with branches of thoughtfulness, generosity, and good intentions. With the next deed — as she listened compassionately to the plight of the Yidden — more and more chesed grew inside of her until she found it in her heart to save the entire family. The tree continued to blossom as other trees were planted, and over the next six years, it flourished into an entire forest of self-sacrifice and goodwill. It is hard to measure her reward.

All stemming from one kind act of opening the door for a despairing, sick woman.

The Gift of Giving

Sometimes, Hashem uses the most seemingly random encounters to transform the lives of those involved. In regard to the life of Rav Avraham Yeshaya Heber, the founder of Matnas Chaim, Gift of Life — a kidney-donor organization in Eretz Yisrael — that was most certainly the case.

RAV AVRAHAM YESHAYA NEVER PLANNED ON CREATING such an organization. An outstanding *talmid chacham,* in his younger years he was a rebbi in a yeshivah and a rav. He left his mark on individuals and families and was dear to everyone who knew him. He thought this was to be his career; he didn't seem cut out for anything else. After all, he had the training, and he had the knowledge; he had learned in Ponovezh for many years.

But when Rav Avraham Yeshaya turned 42, everything changed. He hadn't been feeling well for a while and one day, he felt particularly lethargic. He was walking in the street when he began feeling woozy and then he fainted. Ambulances rushed to the scene. He was revived and then transported to the hospital. After a thorough examination, Rav Avraham Yeshaya was given the devastating news — his kidneys were not working properly. He began receiving dialysis three times a week, which drained him of his energy and left him exhausted, unable to accomplish much. What he desperately needed was a donor kidney. But for the meantime, his life was on pause.

Or so he thought.

One day, while receiving his dialysis treatment, Rav Avraham Yeshaya met a 19-year-old boy, Pinchas Turgeman, who had been born with defective kidneys. While still a child, he had received a transplant and remained fairly healthy, while taking a strict regimen of pills to make sure his body would not reject the foreign kidney. But one day, when he was 16, a dreadful tragedy occurred. His brother Yair was killed by a group of terrorists. While the entire family was devastated, Pinchas, who was extremely close to his brother, took the loss especially hard. His mood took a turn for the worse, and over the next several weeks, he stopped taking his daily pills. Without his medication, his kidney began to falter. Although it had worked beautifully for years, his body began rejecting it. There was no undoing the process. Pinchas was in need of another kidney, and for now, he was on dialysis.

When Pinchas first met Rav Avraham Yeshaya in the dialysis center, they made small talk and Pinchas felt himself uplifted by Rav Avraham Yeshaya's sparkling personality. Not only that, but soon Rav Avraham Yeshaya began to learn with the young man and before long, they'd established a brand-new "yeshivah," right there in the dialysis ward! The two of them were the first registered *talmidim*. They scheduled their treatments to coincide with each other, and with each treatment, they learned more and more, *sugya* after *sugya*. The *blatt* piled up and the yeshivah was a huge success.

But they both needed a *yeshuah*.

After one year, good news arrived; a kidney was found for Rav Avraham Yeshaya. Thrilled, he prepared for his transplant but continued to learn and lend encouragement to Pinchas. A short time later, he underwent the operation and it was a success. Although he needed time to recover, from the moment he received his new kidney, Rav Avraham Yeshaya was determined to find one for his *chavrusa,* Pinchas.

Though he was not a full-blown organization, merely a one-man operation, Rav Avraham Yeshaya networked and made phone calls, hoping to find a match. He printed up signs and hung them everywhere. Shuls. Supermarkets. Streetlamps. Everywhere.

Although his initial search came up empty, there were signs of encouragement and *chizuk* along the way. One day, he received a phone call from an 87-year-old woman who wanted to volunteer. Though she was not a viable kidney donor, in her words, "Everyone needs to do the most they can. I may not be able to donate a kidney, but I can donate my *tefillos*." Wow! Rav Avraham Yeshaya was blown away by her caring and kindness, and he gave her Pinchas' name so she could daven for him.

The search intensified and Rav Avraham Yeshaya left no stone unturned. He tried to get others to help and spread the word that a 19-year-old boy was in desperate need of a kidney. Finally, after a number of months, a donor was found. Immediately, Pinchas began the necessary testing to determine if the kidney was a proper match and if he would be able to withstand the rigors of the transplant operation. All systems were go but as the date of the transplant neared, Pinchas' strength began to ebb away. He died a few days before the scheduled transplant.

But on the day he died, Matnas Chaim, Gift of Life, was born. Rav Avraham Yeshaya was determined to dedicate his life to help others in need of kidneys, to help them find a match. And with that, he transformed the industry. By the time of his death, 800 individuals in Eretz Yisrael had received the "Gift of Life," a new kidney to give them a new lease on life. Viewed as a national hero, Rav Heber received numerous awards and was lauded for his extraordinary work and dedication.

Tragically, soon after the coronavirus struck, on April 23, 2020, Rav Avraham Yeshaya Heber rejoined his *chavrusa*, Pinchas, in the *Yeshivah shel Maalah*.

Yet the lifesaving organization he founded continues to give the gift of life.

Please Listen to Their Pleas

AS A MOTHER OF A LARGE FAMILY, WITH MANY CHILDREN and grandchildren, Bracha tried to ignore the symptoms that begged for her attention, especially the lethargy; no matter how much she tried to rest, she never seemed to regain her strength. Then there were the fevers, which lingered longer than for most flus, as well as the constant achiness. Though she didn't like going to doctors, after a while she realized she had no choice. The physician, Dr. Shafrir, ran a series of tests, did a thorough workup, and told Bracha he would be in touch. While speaking to him, Bracha picked up the veiled nuances. Although he tried to hide it, it was obvious he was concerned.

A few days later, Bracha received a phone call. Dr. Shafrir wanted to speak to her and asked that her husband, Binyamin, attend the meeting. That was a giveaway. A husband isn't needed when you have a vitamin D deficiency or your zinc levels are a bit low. Immediately, a pit formed in her stomach. Something was seriously wrong.

Dr. Shafrir sat across from Binyamin and Bracha. She could have predicted exactly what he was going to say: There was a mass. It would have to be removed surgically and then, in all probability, she was going to need chemotherapy and radiation.

While listening to what he said, all Bracha could think about was her children. As silly as it seemed, in her mind, she was wondering how she would tell them the news in a way that would not worry them. Yes, they were now grown-ups, but they were still children, her children, and she was their mother. Although she was sick, she had no intention of relinquishing her job.

But that should have been the least of her worries. A week later, Binyamin and Bracha entered the hospital early in the morning, and the doctors performed an eight-hour surgery to remove the growth. This was followed by a few rounds of chemotherapy and radiation, plus a variety of some other treatments.

Yet her condition worsened by the day.

She wasn't responding to the treatments and at no point did her cancer go into remission. In a matter of a few months, Bracha had lost all her strength, along with her ability to function normally. Although the doctors tried different treatments, nothing worked. Finally, one day, Dr. Shafrir called her and her husband into the office.

Another husband-wife meeting, where he apologized for his straightforwardness but wanted them to know that they had exhausted all their options. The cancer was very aggressive. Though Dr. Shafrir and his team had hoped to slow its growth, if not eradicate it, nothing had worked. He recommended that they go home and get their affairs in order.

It was a matter of days at most.

The children came over to say goodbye. One by one, they entered their mother's room and with aching hearts, hugged and kissed their mother goodbye. It was a heartrending scene. Binyamin did his best to hold everyone together. His wife was dying and his children were crushed. There would be time later for him to mourn, but for now, he was trying to take care of his family.

That night, as Bracha's strength began to leave her, the children took turns sitting in the room. It was a long night, with muffled cries and lots of tissues and *Tehillim*.

Before daybreak, Binyamin realized he would be best off davening first thing in the morning. He anticipated a period of *aninus* (after the passing of an immediate relative when one is prohibited from doing any mitzvos), and he wanted to daven as soon as the opportunity presented itself. At that point, nothing was imminent, so he knew he could leave his wife for an hour, even though she was slipping in and out of consciousness. In addition, his children were all there. He went to daven, where he begged one last time for a miracle.

When he returned, his wife was sitting up in bed with a weak but discernible smile.

Yes, it was a miracle.

He ran to her bedside, wondering how this could have happened. Bracha took a sip of water and began to tell her story. Her words were clear, but she spoke slowly, to catch her breath every so often. The entire family sat at the edge of their seats, hanging onto her every word.

> *As you know, Abba and I and our baby girl Rivka were in Chevron in 1929 when a gruesome slaughter took place. Close to seventy men, women, and children were butchered by axe-wielding Arabs, crazed with hatred and bloodlust for Jews. It was a terrible, terrible time. Though the three of us were miraculously saved, another couple was not so fortunate. Nebach, they were murdered, but somehow, their baby daughter, Penina, survived. With no one to feed or care for her, Penina, too, almost died.*
>
> *After her weak body was discovered, the search was on for someone to take in this little orphan and feed her. As a new mother, I was able to feed her. Thus, even though I was taking care of my own baby, I took her in as my own. And that's what your father and I did during the most turbulent and tumultuous period of our lives.*
>
> *After I fed her and cared for her for several months, she was taken in by a relative.*

Now Bracha explained how this connected to the here and now. "Last night, as I was slipping away, I was given a peek into the *Olam HaEmes*, where Penina's parents begged for my life. 'This is the woman who had such *rachmanus* on our little girl when she was crying for her mother. Look, her children are crying now for their mother. Where is the *rachmanus*?' The *Beis Din shel Maalah* accepted their plea and ripped up my *gzar din*. I will be able to live."

After sharing this riveting tale, Rav Chizkiyahu Mishkovsky remarked, "So many years had passed since that story took place in Chevron. Over half of a century! The woman probably did not often think about that act of compassion and kindness."

But it wasn't forgotten.

Scrolls of Salvation

During the war years, thousands of Jews fled from Poland, Lithuania, Russia, Ukraine, and other Nazi-occupied countries to Uzbekistan, a country in Central Asia. Some traveled alone but others went in groups.

AS ONE GROUP OF FAMILIES GATHERED THEIR BELONGings and prepared to escape, they sent someone to the shul to retrieve two Sifrei Torah from the *aron*. Had they left them behind, the scrolls would have been destroyed by the Nazis. Wrapped in *talleisim*, these Sifrei Torah accompanied them throughout their harrowing escape. At every step of the way, the Jews ensured that not only were their families safe, but the Sifrei Torah were too. When they arrived in Uzbekistan, they placed the Sifrei Torah in the "shul," a small building designated for davening. They offered a special *tefillah* to Hashem, thanking Him for their safe passage and the privilege of protecting the Sifrei Torah.

Or had the Sifrei Torah protected them? They would never know, but it felt comforting knowing that their most prized and treasured possessions were safe and secure.

The families eventually dispersed and made their way to their new homes, some in America, others in Eretz Yisrael. A number even went toward Siberia. As they left, family by family, the Sifrei Torah were left behind in Uzbekistan. Though the Uzbeks didn't love the Jews, they had nowhere near the same vitriolic animosity toward the Jews as did the Nazis; the Sifrei Torah were in no danger. Or so they thought.

One day, the non-Jews of the village went to empty the synagogue so they could turn it into a social hall; after all, nobody was davening there anymore. But when they opened the *aron* and saw the Sifrei Torah, a deep-rooted dislike surfaced, and the younger crowd relished the thought that they now had the opportunity to burn the holy scrolls. They took the Sifrei Torah outside and began setting up a bonfire. What a sight it would be!

Although the town was almost completely devoid of Jews, one remained: Menashe the shoemaker. When it came to Torah, Menashe was completely ignorant; he didn't even know how to read or write Hebrew. He had never even learned a *pasuk* of Chumash. Yet he possessed a tremendous passion, love, and respect for the Torah.

When Rashid, his non-Jewish neighbor, informed him of the plan to burn the scrolls, Menashe realized he had to take action. But what could a little shoemaker do against a mob of crazed hoodlums looking to destroy anything Jewish? Though Menashe was powerless, Rashid, the largest, strongest, and toughest man in the village, was not. Menashe approached his neighbor with the request to salvage the scrolls. "What will you give me in return?" was Rashid's response.

Menashe thought quickly. He didn't have much in terms of materialism. However, he knew that if he offered Rashid a blessing, he would grab it. Rashid, a religious man, had been taught by his mother the *koach* of a Jewish blessing. Rashid never forgot that lesson.

They struck an agreement and immediately Rashid went to retrieve the scrolls. At first, the riled-up crowd refused to hand them over. But with his brute strength, Rashid cast the ruffians aside, grabbed the scrolls, and brought them back to Menashe.

Seeing his neighbor coming, Menashe ran to retrieve the Sifrei Torah. He held onto them and danced with them like it was Simchas Torah. Perhaps he wasn't the biggest scholar, but his love for Torah was without limits.

Then he came through with his part of the deal. He blessed Rashid with long life and prosperity, plus an additional, more personal, blessing: that Rashid and his wife should merit a child who would grow up to be a fine man. Rashid and his wife had always wanted a child, but had not yet been blessed with one.

Rashid and his wife were not the only ones to be blessed.

Menashe and his wife also did not have children after many years of marriage. Apparently, though, his *berachah* carried a boomerang effect and worked for him, as well. Soon after saving the Sifrei Torah, Menashe and his wife were blessed with twins.

In time, along with the Sifrei Torah, he and his family made their way to Eretz Yisrael, where his children returned to their roots. All his descendants are *shomrei Torah*, and his five grandsons are working as *sofrim*, writing more Sifrei Torah.

Go figure. One man, who couldn't even read a pasuk of Chumash, had a burning desire to protect the Torah from destruction. Hashem placed that desire into his children and grandchildren, who developed their own love of Torah.

Menashe's one act of devotion and dedication will pay dividends until the end of time.

Look at how far one noble deed can carry you.

The Plot of the Story

According to Jewish law, we must do our utmost to maintain the dignity of every individual, both in life and in death. The chevrah kaddisha, the holy burial society, treats the body with reverence and exceptional care, and great caution is taken to preserve the honor of the meis. Since the Torah strictly forbids autopsies, askanim are often called forth to prevent any such desecration of the guf. Unfortunately, in the 1950s and 1960s and even into the 1970s, the Israeli government approved of the performance of autopsies.

RAV KALMAN EHRLICHMAN, A *TALMID* OF THE BAAL HaSulam, Rav Yehuda Ashlag, was *niftar* in 1966, when the battle against autopsies was still raging in Eretz Yisrael. After he died, the coroner refused to release Rav Kalman's body. Waiting for a release form, the hospital held the body for a day and a half. As the hours wore on, the threat of an autopsy grew more and more real. Family, friends, and *talmidim* tried every avenue, but the hospital administration refused to release the body.

Eventually, they realized that the authorities could be convinced to give in, but it would have to be through unorthodox means. Rav Yechezkel Yosef Ashlag, a grandson of the Baal HaSulam, collected large sums of money and bribed the officials in charge to "look the other way." Ultimately, he succeeded in securing the release of Rav Kalman's body and giving him a proper Jewish burial on Har HaMenuchos, near the burial place of his rebbi, the Baal HaSulam.

That night, Rav Kalman appeared to Rav Yechezkel Yosef in a dream. Startled, Rav Yechezkel Yosef asked Rav Kalman what he wanted. He responded, "How can I repay you for your kindness? If not for you, there is no telling what would have happened.

In all probability, those in charge would have tried to perform an autopsy on me, *Rachmana litzlan*. But even if they would not have succeeded, it would have caused me terrible pain and aggravation, as days would have passed until they released my body. So tell me, what can I do for you?"

Rav Yechezkel Yosef claimed he did what anyone else would have done. He had acted *le'Sheim Shamayim* and wanted nothing in return. Rav Kalman was adamant about repaying him, though. "I give my word that I am going to facilitate something special for you."

Suddenly, Rav Yechezkel Yosef woke up. He thought it was an interesting dream, but after being occupied with the burial and its attendant details over the past 24-plus hours, it made sense that he had dreamt about it, as well.

The story was all but forgotten.

Five decades passed. In time, Rav Yechezkel Yosef became the Rebbe of Ashlag (the Chassidus goes by its founder's last name, not his city) and influenced many to grow in their learning and *yiras Shamayim*.

On the 4th of Av, 2016, Rav Yechezkel Yosef was *niftar*. When the Baal HaSulam passed away in 1955, his *talmidim* purchased forty to fifty plots near him to be used for family and Chassidim. But now, though the members of the *chevrah kaddisha* checked the map of Har HaMenuchos over and over, they could not find even one empty plot. Nevertheless, one of the members of the *chevrah kaddisha* went to Har HaMenuchos and examined the area himself, and he saw that, somehow, one plot was still open.

Upon further investigation, it was discovered that this plot had been purchased many years earlier for a father and son. The father died first and was buried in his spot. When his son passed away, however, his family was unaware that this plot had been designated for him and buried him elsewhere. Which meant that this plot was open.

They looked at the *matzeivah* of the father.

Rav Kalman Ehrlichman.

Rav Kalman kept his promise. Rav Yechezkel Yosef was buried right next to Rav Kalman. The debt from 50 years earlier had been repaid.

One act of chesed shel emes that will last an eternity.

One Little Goat

Rav Eliyahu Diskin, a mashpia in Eretz Yisrael, recounted a story that took place some 20 years ago.

NOT FAR FROM HIS HOUSE IN YERUSHALAYIM, THERE was a yeshivah called Shavei Golah (returnees of the exile), a yeshivah comprised mostly of young Russian *olim* who had become *baalei teshuvah*. Every Shabbos, some of the young men joined the Diskin family for one of the Shabbos meals. One of those fine young men once asked if he could bring his family members from Haifa, who were completely unobservant. He wanted to expose them to the beauty of the life he had chosen.

Obviously, the boy's family wouldn't be able to come for Shabbos. Instead, the Diskins invited them for a Melaveh Malkah, and the invitation was graciously accepted. The Diskins decorated the table beautifully and welcomed their guests, including the young man's elderly grandfather; he was nearly 85 years old and had only recently arrived from Russia.

As the Diskins and their guests began to converse, it became evident that though the young man's parents were not observant, they seemed to know some of the basics. But the grandfather knew absolutely nothing. The Communists had done an excellent job eradicating religion from the Jewish people, including this individual, who was just a young boy when they had come into power in Russia.

Rav Eliyahu wanted to include the elderly man in the conversation, so he began to speak about Judaism to see what he was familiar with. Immediately, Rav Eliyahu sensed a flicker of interest in the grandfather. However, the man had no memories. Rav Eliyahu asked him about Abraham, Isaac, and Jacob. But the old man stared back blankly. When Rav Eliyahu mentioned Moses and David, he received the same uncomprehending stare.

Bereishis, Shemos, Vayikra, Bamidbar, and *Devarim*. Still no response. It seemed like it was the first time the man was hearing any of these concepts. What a tragedy it was, an almost 85-year-old being introduced to Judaism for the very first time.

Next, Rav Eliyahu tried to trigger the man's memory by asking the man if he remembered something about the Jewish holidays. Perhaps he had some recollection of those memorable times. Did he know anything about the giving of the Torah? Leaving Egypt? The Tabernacle?

Shabbos, Rosh Hashanah, Yom Kippur, Succos, Chanukah?

Nothing.

Shabbos candles, shofar, *Ne'ilah*, *arba'ah minim*, menorah?

Though desperate to find something, anything, Rav Eliyahu became worried that perhaps he had asked too many questions. Maybe he should just let the matter go. Even so, he found it hard to imagine that a man in his mid-80s knew nothing at all about Judaism. Somehow, he sensed that there must be something to ignite a spark in the man's dormant soul. So he kept going.

At that point, Rav Eliyahu brought up Pesach: the Seder and matzah and *maror*. He even mentioned the Four Questions, then slowly went through various snippets of the *Haggadah — Ha Lachma Anya... Mah Nishtanah... Avadim Hayinu...* up until the end of the *Haggadah*.

Still nothing. All hope seemed lost.

Finally, he came to the very end of the *Haggadah* and began to sing *Chad Gadya*. By now, Rav Eliyahu had exhausted all his options. He felt as if he were singing the song more for himself than for anyone else.

Suddenly, he heard a cry.

"*Ein tzigele*! *Ein tzigele*! One little goat! One little goat!"

The spark had been ignited. A memory had been awakened.

Now, the elderly man began to retrace his steps. As if going back in time, he traveled backward through the *Haggadah*, while simultaneously discovering the lost memories trapped for so many years. Ultimately, he worked his way all the way to the beginning. Unbelievably, he remembered the Seder from when he was just 4 years old!

Moreover, this enabled him to begin his journey back home. Rav Eliyahu started learning with him, and the man began spending more and more time in yeshivah. Soon, the old man was donning *tefillin* and contemplating keeping Shabbos.

He became a *baal teshuvah* at the age of 84!

One year later, the elderly man passed away, returning his soul to Heaven as a complete *shomer Torah u'mitzvos*.

One little goat! *Ein tzigele*!

Look at the strength of the Jewish people. Look at the strength of our faith.

There will be times when we feel we are down to our very last glimmer. But the flame will never fade completely.

As Jews, we possess an indomitable spirit, a light that will never be extinguished.

ONE GOOD WORD

More Talking, Less Sandwich

The following two stories are from the most powerful stories in this book. Interestingly, both of these memorable episodes took place in the same location, a sandwich shop.

"A sandwich shop?" you may ask. What can possibly happen in a sandwich shop that would be life-altering?

Read the stories and decide for yourself.

YITZI, A *YUNGERMAN,* WAS LEARNING IN AN OUT-OF-TOWN kollel. He loved his learning, and he and his wife were so pleased to start off their marriage immersed in Torah. However, he did not come from a wealthy home, nor did his wife. After several years, their funds began to dwindle. The time had come to move back to his hometown so Yitzi could find a job and support his family.

Without any real training or experience, it was not easy to find a job. After only six months, Yitzi found himself drowning in a huge hole of debt. He knew he had to find a job quickly, or he would sink into too great a hole to dig his way out of.

One day, as inglorious as it sounds, Yitzi walked into Sendy's Sandwiches, the local kosher sandwich shop, and asked if he could work behind the counter. As a proud *ben Torah* and *yeshivahman,* this was a difficult step. He certainly never envisioned himself working at a sandwich shop. Not that there's anything wrong with it — it's an honest way to make a living — but since he was going to be around many people in the community whom he knew well, it wasn't ideal for him. He hoped it would tide him over for a few months until something better came along.

In spite of its name, Sendy's was not exclusively for sandwiches. It also sold other prepared food items, especially for Shabbos, such as cholent, kugel, chopped liver, gefilte fish, salads, and herring. In fact, on Erev Shabbos the store didn't sell sandwiches at all. They were just too busy to make sandwiches, a process that usually takes time.

One Friday, as many customers came in asking for their Shabbos orders, Sendy's Sandwich Shop was becoming more hectic by the moment. In the meantime, a very successful and wealthy fellow walked into the store. Talking and texting on his phone, he barely looked up when he ordered his usual, a corned-beef sandwich, to go, with his Shabbos order. Trying to fill many orders at one time, Yitzi apologized and told the man that on Fridays the store did not make sandwiches. But the customer was none too pleased.

He asked — no, demanded — his corned-beef sandwich. When Yitzi repeated that they don't make sandwiches on Friday, the man looked at him in a very demeaning manner and asked, "Do I need to get the boss here, or are you gonna make me a sandwich?"

Yitzi knew that the customer and his boss, Sendy, were good friends and he wasn't looking to make any waves, but the tone and the comment stung. Furthermore, with a store filled with customers, he was very embarrassed. But as he begrudgingly made the sandwich, the traffic in the store slowed to a halt and before long, Sendy's was completely empty except for Yitzi and the customer. Still hurt by the comment, he looked up from the sandwich and addressed his arrogant customer.

"I just want you to know something. I didn't always dream of being a sandwich maker. I'm just a few months removed from learning in an out-of-town kollel. Soon after leaving kollel, I found myself in heavy debt. Since I don't come from a wealthy family and I didn't marry into one, I decided to work here for a few months so I can keep my head above water, or at least just beneath it, as I look for a real job."

Still busily texting on his phone, the customer took a moment to glare at Yitzi. Then he tossed carelessly, "And why exactly are you telling me this?"

Yitzi wasn't a wimp and he wasn't particularly sensitive, but he felt like crying. Feeling extremely vulnerable, he told the well-to-do man in the most conciliatory tone he could muster, "I was hoping that if you better understood my circumstances, perhaps it would change our relationship and the way you interact with me."

In a dismissive and biting tone, the man snapped, "How about a little less talking and a little more sandwich?"

Yitzi was so incredibly humiliated he could barely breathe.

That is story number one, a horrible one at that.

But in that very same sandwich shop, an angelic individual, Reb Boruch, acted in the opposite manner. Instead of belittling Yitzi, he lifted him up and raised his spirits in a way Yitzi never thought possible.

One day, Reb Boruch, an older and very well-respected man in the community, walked into Sendy's. This story also took place on a Friday, but a quiet one. He asked for a few items and Yitzi, always with a cheerful disposition and upbeat attitude, packed up his items and wished him well. Before leaving, Reb Boruch, whom Yitzi did not recognize, struck up a conversation with Yitzi. It was filled with positivity and encouragement, and Yitzi soaked it all up.

On the following week, Reb Boruch came back and the scenario repeated itself. The order was relatively small, the conversation anything but — at least to Yitzi. Reb Boruch shared a *dvar*

Torah and asked about Yitzi's well-being and the well-being of his family. As the weeks went by, Reb Boruch's visit was something Yitzi looked forward to. It was only one customer and it wasn't a very long conversation, but it was extremely uplifting and meaningful to Yitzi.

About a year and a half later, Reb Boruch was sitting *shivah* for his father. Yitzi, who had since found himself a different job, made a point of being *menachem avel*; he felt such gratitude to Reb Boruch. While there, he told Reb Boruch's son how Reb Boruch appeared out of nowhere one day in Sendy's Sandwich Shop, and must have really liked the food because he came back every week, and always with a positive word and an uplifting smile.

As soon as Yitzi finished telling his tale, Reb Boruch's son began to cry. "Now let me tell you the story behind your story. One Friday about a year and a half ago, my father came home and told me how he'd walked into Sendy's Sandwich Shop, looked at the guy behind the counter, and seen that he needed a pick-me-up. And so, even though he never needed the food, he made it his business to visit you every week for one reason and one reason only, to give encouragement and *chizuk* to another Yid who could use it."

Yitzi could barely breathe, but this time because he was so incredibly moved.

One sandwich shop.

Two customers.

Two conversations.

One of them built an individual.

The other nearly destroyed him.

Today, Yitzi is a successful businessman, who makes more than enough to support himself and his family. But that's not enough. He does everything within his power to help others stand on their feet, as well.

Hanging in his office is a big sign. Most have no idea what it means. But for Yitzi, it's all the motivation he needs, a reminder of how to treat others and the difference a good or bad word can make.

"How about a little less talking and a little more sandwich?"

A Perfect Set

During the shivah for Rav Chaim Greineman, nephew and talmid muvhak of the Chazon Ish, a woman from the north of Eretz Yisrael walked into the Greineman home. As she sat there, numerous people came and went, offering their wishes of condolence and nechamah, though nobody seemed to recognize her. Finally, someone in the family asked her why she was there. She cleared her throat and shared her poignant tale.

MY HUSBAND PASSED AWAY MANY YEARS AGO, WHEN I was only a young woman with a house full of children. Not only did my children not have a father, but we had no money either. We were very, very poor, relying on handouts to make it from week to week.

When Succos arrived, things became even more difficult. There were extra expenses, but no extra money to be found. I needed to dress the children in new clothes, choose and purchase the *arba'ah minim*, erect a *succah*, and procure and cook lots of food.

Realizing our dire situation, my daughter offered to find an afterschool babysitting job to cover one set of *arba'ah minim*. I sent my teenaged son, Naftali, who was learning in Bnei Brak, to purchase the set near his yeshivah.

He walked over to the *mocher*, the *esrog* merchant, handed him an envelope with the money, and asked for a set. The seasoned seller opened the envelope, peered inside, and informed Naftali that while the money was enough to buy one of the *minim*, it would not cover an entire set. Distraught, Naftali revealed that he had no more money. The *mocher* apologized that he was unable to sell him a set for that price and returned the envelope so Naftali could try his luck elsewhere. With the store full of potential buyers, the seller couldn't pay much more attention to the young boy. Obviously, he had no idea about my child's background. He had no way of knowing that my son didn't have a father.

Disappointed and dejected, Naftali walked out with nothing more than a broken heart. Afraid to embarrass himself further and enter another store, he wandered the streets. A few hours passed. Meanwhile, a kind man took note of the teenager walking around aimlessly and asked him what he was looking for. After Naftali spilled his tale of woe, the man directed him to Rechov Yerushalayim. "When you get there, ask for the home of Rav Chaim Greineman. He sells *arba'ah minim*; maybe he will be able to help you." Apparently, the man hoped Rav Greineman would pick up on Naftali's sad situation and make it work for him.

Which is precisely what happened. However, it was the way Rav Greineman did it that was so special. As soon as Naftali walked through the door of the Greineman home, Rav Chaim immediately noticed him and struck up a conversation, which in itself was noteworthy, as he was busy with an apartment full of customers. Why would he pay attention to Naftali? But he did.

Naftali told him he was learning in a local *mosad* and wanted to buy *arba'ah minim*. Rav Greineman asked why Naftali didn't just use his father's *arba'ah minim*. Remember that in those days it wasn't a given for *bachurim* to have their own set. It was a rarity.

Naftali burst out crying. "Because my father is in Gan Eden!" He couldn't get a hold of himself. Rav Chaim felt terrible. But he didn't let the moment pass without doing something about it. Immediately, he got down to business. "Yes, I sell *lulavim* and *esrogim*. However, I'm not taking money from you."

Naftali grew uncomfortable. "Why?" he asked. "Because I'm a *yasom*?"

Rav Greineman clarified, "No, I only charge those who are working. I don't take money from someone like you who learns Torah. Because the world stands on your shoulders!"

That moment was valuable to Naftali. Rav Greineman didn't make him feel like a *nebach'l*. He didn't remind him that he was a poor *yasom*. Instead, he built him up and made him feel like he was deserving of this privilege.

Rav Chaim took Naftali's money and handed him a beautiful set of *arba'ah minim*. Naftali came home and delightedly displayed each part to all of us. Every day of Yom Tov, he walked to shul with the set and proudly marched around during *Hoshanos*.

When Succos was over, Rav Chaim continued to maintain a *shaychus* with Naftali and kept track of him in yeshivah.

The woman finished her story and everyone in the room was inspired once more to hear of the gadlus of Rav Chaim, who knew how to build a young man with wisdom and kindness, rather than a display of pity.

The right word at the right time.

One Conversation

CHAIM LOST HIS FATHER, YAAKOV, WHEN HE WAS VERY young. Chanah, his widowed mother, had a very difficult time making it on her own in Yerushalayim of the 1940s. Supporting her son Chaim did not come easy. To complicate matters for the young *almanah*, Chaim was a very weak student, at the bottom third of his class. It took until the age of 12 for Chaim to finally learn how to read and chant the *pesukim* in the traditional singsong. However, he still didn't understand a word he was saying and couldn't translate even one *pasuk* of Chumash.

Chanah felt sorry for Chaim; she didn't want him to feel like a failure. Perhaps it would be best to spare him the embarrassment and shame associated with school, and apprentice him to a carpenter or a blacksmith. This would also alleviate the financial burden resting heavily on her shoulders.

Chanah discussed her idea with some of the women in the neighborhood, who knew her and her son, and knew that Chaim was not much of a student. Most of them agreed with her assessment and encouraged her to find someone to teach him a trade. But one woman, the wife of Rav Simcha Zissel Shapiro, a well-known Yid in Yerushalayim, thought otherwise. She told her friend that she did not disagree with the idea altogether, but pointed out that Chaim was only 12 years old, not yet bar mitzvah. "Imagine how embarrassed he will be when everyone else his age is still in school and he's already gone to work, even before his bar mitzvah. Why don't you wait out the year? When he turns 13 you can send him to work."

Chanah mulled it over and decided her friend had a point. She would give Chaim another year.

Over the next year, he began to show slight signs of improvement. He was able to read, translate, and understand one *parashah,* though he was still far behind the other boys in his yeshivah.

But Chaim was determined. And his mother decided to wait a bit longer.

In Yeshivas Tiferes Tzvi, Chaim had a hard time finding *chavrusos.* The other boys were afraid he would cause them to lag behind. But Chaim would not be denied. He refused to give up. He was determined to grow and to *shteig.*

Eventually, Chaim transferred to Yeshivas Slabodka in Bnei Brak. Though he worked diligently and learned every spare moment, he still had trouble finding learning partners, as he struggled to understand the *sugya*. As he would recount later, in Slabodka they used to say, "It's easier to learn with a *shtender* than to learn with Chaim."

Most would have buckled. But not Chaim.

He had one advantage over almost everyone else. He was the biggest *masmid* in the yeshivah. His *hasmadah* was so great that he wore out the paint on the benches where he sat and learned; he never left his seat. He switched back and forth from learning *be'iyun* (in depth) to learning *bekius* (covering ground), hoping that one of the styles would stick with him. But he had no such luck.

In time, though, he began to slowly move forward. Inch by inch, *blatt* by *blatt,* Chaim kept growing in his learning.

After his marriage, Chaim went to learn in the Mir in Yerushalayim. At the time, Rav Chaim Shmulevitz, who later became the rosh yeshivah, was seeking a *chavrusa* who was a *masmid* but not necessarily the biggest *baal kisharon* (most gifted learner). Looking to hone his *hasbarah* (explanation) and elucidation skills, Rav Shmulevitz wanted someone who didn't grasp the material the first time, so he would be forced to explain the material and clarify it for him. The *yungerman*, Chaim, was the perfect candidate, for though he had made enormous strides in his learning, it still required extensive effort and he didn't comprehend the *sugya* the first time around. And so, they began having a learning session together.

At that time, Rav Leizer Yudel Finkel, the rosh yeshivah, asked Chaim to learn also with a newcomer, an American boy from Chicago with vast potential who was not yet up to par. He knew Chaim possessed an extraordinary love for Torah and it would rub off on the raw newcomer.

The boy's name was Nosson Tzvi.

Chaim accepted the challenge and the two developed an unusual rapport. Rav Leizer Yudel loved Chaim, and the two of them loved the young Chicagoan. Not only did Chaim and Nosson

Tzvi learn every moment of every day — *bein hasedarim*, weekends, and *bein hazmanim* included — but Chaim taught Nosson Tzvi Yiddish and Ivrit, as he was a novice in both.

The boy who couldn't *teitch* a *pasuk* in Chumash was now mentoring a protege. And he himself continued to *shteig* and grow and advance in his learning. Years later, Rav Leizer Yudel expressed that the establishment of Yeshivas Mir was worthwhile for a *talmid* such as Rav Chaim Kamil, who would go on to become the rosh yeshivah of Yeshivas Ofakim, alongside Rav Shimshon Pincus.

Decades later, Rav Nosson Tzvi Finkel, the Mirrer rosh yeshivah who transformed Yeshivas Mir into an epicenter of Torah learning with thousands of *talmidim,* referred to Rav Chaim Kamil as his *rebbi muvhak,* to whom he owed his development and his *ahavas haTorah*.

And the world owes its inspiration for *ahavas haTorah* in no small part to Rav Nosson Tzvi.

This inspiring story of grit and perseverance lends hope and encouragement to every bachur who has ever struggled with learning.

But there is perhaps a bigger lesson to be learned.

Rav Chaim Kamil told this story to a bachur who had recently become engaged to a granddaughter of Rav Simcha Zissel Shapiro. "We owe it all to your kallah's grandmother," he told the chassan.

One conversation altered the trajectory of a 12-year-old's schooling, and the Torah world's love for Torah was transformed forever.

Sheli ve'shelachem shelah hu.

Who Laughs Last

Although he was one of the busiest people in the Jewish world, there was one thing Chacham Ovadiah Yosef always made time for. If someone, anyone, wrote a sefer, or even a small kuntrus, and asked him for a haskamah (an approbation), he always agreed to give it. In fact, it's possible that some people wrote kuntrussen just to receive a glowing letter of recommendation from the chacham.

It seemed a bit of a waste of his time. After all, the biggest, best, and brightest minds immersed themselves in his groundbreaking sefarim, such as Yabia Omer, Yechaveh Daas, and Chazon Ovadiah. Was this seemingly endless stream of haskamos for those looking for praise the best way for the gadol hador, who was so careful not to take away even a moment from his learning, to spend his time?

Someone very close to the chacham asked him this question, and he responded with a memorable story.

WHEN HE WAS 17 YEARS OLD AND STILL A *BACHUR*, Ovadiah published the first volume of *Yabia Omer*, on *Maseches Horayos*. Although he felt very good about his publication and *gedolim* approved it, extolling it with high praise, some young men in Ovadiah's yeshivah were jealous and teased young Ovadiah about its content.

It's true that he was only 17, but he was a brilliant boy and this was a monumental piece of work. Nevertheless, the constant derision and degrading comments began wearing away at his confidence, as well as his standing in the yeshivah. One day, when someone asked a strong question in middle of the *shiur*, one of his main detractors mocked Ovadiah publicly and in a sarcastic and cynical tone called out, "Maybe ask the question to the *mechaber* of *Yabia Omer*. Ask 'Chacham' Ovadiah. He knows everything." Of course, Ovadiah was not yet known as a chacham. The cruel young man just intended to tear him down.

At that moment, the barrage of jealous comments finally took their toll. Visibly embarrassed and upset, Ovadiah ran out of the room and out of the yeshivah. He walked past his neighbor, Rav Shimshon Aharon Polansky, the Tepliker Rav, who stopped him and asked what was wrong.

Ovadiah related the entire story: the *sefer* he wrote, the jealousy it stirred up, the fun his peers poked at him. He needed validation and encouragement.

He would find it.

The Tepliker Rav spoke with authority and confidence. "Listen to me, Ovadiah. You are *asid le'gadlus*! You have greatness in your future! You are going to become a *talmid chacham* and a *gadol be'Yisrael*. This *sefer* is only the beginning. Don't pay any attention to the naysayers. They are just envious that you put out an excellent *sefer*. We will see who laughs last."

The rav had a good eye for future *poskim*. Rav Shlomo Zalman Auerbach, Rav Yosef Shalom Elyashiv, Rav Shmuel Wosner, and yes, Chacham Ovadiah Yosef, would all receive *shimush* (practical conduct in *rabbanus*) from him.

The young Sephardic genius went on to become the leader of Sephardic Jewry and the one to restore its crown to its glory.

Chacham Ovadiah finished his story and highlighted, "This is the reason I give a nice haskamah to every kuntrus. I shudder to think what would have happened had I not met Rav Shimshon Aharon, who gave me the encouragement I needed. I never want a mechaber to doubt himself or feel his sefer is unworthy in any way."

Upon hearing this story, two thoughts hit me. First, look what one word of positivity and encouragement can do to the psyche of a fragile bachur, even a gifted one, a mechaber sefarim at a young age. Second, had Ovadiah not met Rav Shimshon Aharon on the way out of the yeshivah, who knows what might have happened; that anonymous bachur's insensitive comment nearly caused irreparable damage to the future of Sephardic Jewry.

We must never underestimate the power of a good word — or a bad one.

A Word of Difference

The outbreak of the coronavirus in 2020, and the subsequent worldwide shutdown, provided challenges for everyone throughout the world, with each individual's challenge unique to his or her circumstances. For example, yeshivah bachurim were uprooted from their environment and given the almost impossible task of creating a small beis midrash inside their homes, where they learned with chavrusos, listened to a shiur on the phone, or learned on their own. For many, the challenge proved too much and they faltered and stumbled along the way.

ARIEL, WHO IS SOMEWHERE IN THE MIDDLE OF A LARGE family of fourteen children, was not as successful in school as the rest of his brothers and sisters. While they have all been stars in terms of scholastic achievement, he was pretty much average. Although his family members have always treated him respectfully, their academic excellence often made him feel incapable and inadequate, which sometimes caused him to not try his best.

When he graduated high school, though Ariel was accepted into a prestigious yeshivah, it was more on his brothers' merit than his own; the administrators assumed he would follow in their footsteps and that he, too, would excel.

Only he didn't.

He struggled every step of the way. *Shiur* was on too high a level and he couldn't — or didn't want to — keep up with his *chavrusos*. While they wanted to learn, Ariel was fine with playing around. After a few years, he decided yeshivah wasn't working for him, and he strongly considered leaving.

Then COVID-19 arrived. While many of the best boys flourished, accepting the challenge at hand and embracing the difficulty as an opportunity for growth, Ariel decided he would drop out. This was as good an excuse as any. Since people were sympathetic to the struggling teenager as a result of the pandemic, now was his chance to leave the yeshivah for good. He would try to find a job.

One day, he was walking the streets of his neighborhood, when he meandered a bit beyond his turf and stepped into a minimarket in the adjacent neighborhood. He supposed a few rugelach and a bottle of soda would help him think.

Sitting behind the cash register was the owner, a man in his 40s, with kind eyes and an effusive personality. "Wow, a *yeshivah bachur*!" he exclaimed. "Your face is *mamash* glowing! Do you know why the entire world is standing? Because of your Torah! Please, let me give you something. I want a small *zechus* in your learning. Take 10 percent off your order and choose an additional three items for free. Anything you want."

Ariel was stunned. This was the first time in his life that anyone had spoken to him in that manner. At home he felt pretty worthless, and in yeshivah it wasn't any better. And now, here, the owner of this *makolet* was treating him like he was someone very special.

Maybe he was.

He decided to give yeshivah another try.

This little exchange made him feel entirely different about himself. He felt more *chashuv* and it began to show in his learning, as well. He carried himself with more pride and stood a bit taller.

In addition, because of the coronavirus, the yeshivah formed "capsules," where groups of *bachurim* remained together for all activities, including davening, learning, eating, and sleeping — without leaving the area at all and with no contact between one capsule and another. In truth, this new and novel arrangement invigorated Ariel and made him feel like he could have a fresh start.

Soon enough, Ariel realized he was a lot smarter than he thought, that when he applied himself he understood the Gemara very well. Before long, he was one of the better boys in the *shiur*.

After the summer *zman* ended, Ariel decided to write a letter to the owner of the minimart and tell him explicitly how much gratitude he felt toward him. In a way, the man had transformed Ariel's life with a few words of encouragement. Ariel took out a pen and paper and began writing, expressing how the storeowner had changed the way he viewed himself, how he would always be grateful for the boost he had received during such a difficult time in his life.

The day before the Elul *zman* began, Ariel walked toward the *makolet*. However, as he was about to enter, a large white sign covering the door stopped him in his tracks. It was the type of sign that's posted when the storeowner is sitting *shivah*.

Nebach, Ariel thought, *he must have lost one of his parents.*

As he read the sign, though, he realized he was wrong. *Oy*! The storeowner himself had died. He had suffered a sudden heart attack and passed away instantly.

Ariel held the letter in his hand as the tears stung his eyes. He checked when the *shivah* was ending and where they were sitting, and decided to deliver the letter to the family of the *niftar*.

But as he began walking toward the house, his phone rang. It had just been announced that his yeshivah was entering the capsule once again and if he didn't arrive soon, the capsule would be closed. He wouldn't be able to get in.

Ariel was torn. He wanted to deliver the letter, to express what the storeowner meant to him. But he couldn't throw away his *zman.*

He ran back to the yeshivah and quickly approached the *menahel* and presented his quandary. The *menahel,* who was not intimately involved in the day-to-day learning and would not be entering the capsule, offered to deliver the letter himself and tell the entire story to the best of his ability. Ariel thanked him, handed him the letter, and entered the capsule.

The *menahel* had noticed Ariel's transformation and was very moved by the entire episode; he did not waste any time in fulfilling his mission. He went to the *shivah* home and handed the *almanah* the letter. She read it and held it close to her heart. With her eyes filled with tears, she proceeded to read it aloud to her children, adding what the *menahel* had shared about Ariel and how much he had changed as a result of the *niftar*'s words. The letter and its message brought the entire family immense *nechamah.*

"I was planning on writing a Sefer Torah in my husband's memory," the widow shared. "However, now I realize that my husband already wrote a Sefer Torah, for there is no more beautiful a Sefer Torah than a boy learning Torah as he should. Furthermore, by causing a boy to stay in yeshivah, it's just like my husband placed the Sefer Torah into the *aron kodesh*!"

Moved and inspired, the *menahel* returned to the yeshivah and relayed all he had witnessed to Ariel. "Do you hear? You're a Sefer Torah!"

Ariel had a very special Elul *zman.* Building on the success of his last *zman,* he blossomed even more and developed a greater desire to learn, along with an even better understanding of his learning. He felt as though Hashem was giving him *kefitzas haderech* (travel between two places in an unnaturally brief amount of time), as he kept growing by leaps and bounds.

One year later, Ariel is the star of his shiur.

But he knows there is work to be done.

There are other stars who just need to know they can shine. And with a word or two of encouragement, he hopes to get them there.

TORAH

Dreams Never Die

Daf Yomi has captivated the hearts and minds of Klal Yisrael, serving as a loyal companion, never leaving its learner's side. Whether one attends a live daily shiur or listens to a recorded one, the virtual explosion of learning Torah as a result of the Daf, especially in the last three or four cycles, has been unprecedented.

There are hundreds of stories of those who commit to Daf Yomi, most telling how it has transformed their lives. Perhaps few stories are more special than the following one, told by Rav Chizkiyahu Mishkovsky, who heard it from his brother Rav Avraham Yitzchak.

AT THE LAST SIYUM HASHAS ON JANUARY 1, 2020, NEARLY 100,000 people came together in MetLife Stadium for the once-in-seven-years' celebration of finishing Shas, with many satellite locations joining from all over the globe. While the *lomdei haDaf*, the learners of the Daf, are the primary honorees, the event has become an opportunity for all of Klal Yisrael to celebrate the beauty and privilege of learning Torah.

Although the main focus of the *siyum* is on Torah learning, there is also a wonderful sentiment of *achdus* and Jewish unity permeating the *siyum* every cycle. This manifests itself the moment the final Amen of the *Kaddish* is recited. The music begins and time after time, spontaneous dancing erupts. It feels as though the entire stadium is shaking with energy, causing strangers to hold onto each other like long-lost brothers.

Not only did thousands come from America for the last few *siyumim,* but large contingents came from other countries, as well. Mexico, which has become a major center of Torah learning, sent a large group of representatives. Among that group at a recent Siyum HaShas was Reb Shimon Elyakun. Sitting next to him was an *eltere Yid,* 90 years old, whom he had never met before. As soon as the dancing began, the two began dancing as if they'd known each other their entire lives. Obviously, the 90-year-old wasn't moving so quickly, but his joy seemed otherworldly. As the music reverberated and the multitudes rejoiced, Reb Shimon's new friend mentioned that he felt a special *simchah* at this moment, like the whole *siyum* was just for him. Reb Shimon couldn't help but notice that the Yid's eyes glistened with tears.

As the man shared his story, Reb Shimon began to understand why.

> *I grew up many years ago in Lublin, the hometown of Rav Meir Shapiro, founder of Daf Yomi. On one Simchas Torah when I was very young, Rav Meir, who was never blessed with children of his own, lifted me onto his shoulders and danced around with great enthusiasm. For Rav Meir, nothing rivaled simchas haTorah. While I held onto his hands, he gave me a berachah, "One day, you will finish Shas!"*
>
> *Though I was overjoyed with the berachah, I was too young to know what it entailed. I had never learned a page of Gemara in my life. But I answered Amen and we continued to dance together.*
>
> *Soon, I began to learn Gemara. The journey had begun.*
>
> *But a few short years later, World War II began and all*

Jewish life came to an abrupt halt; all schools and yeshivos dismantled. I can't begin to describe the horrors my family and I experienced. I lost everyone and endured the shivah medurei Gehinnom, the seven levels of Purgatory. At one point, five of us were trapped in a pit. The Nazis were about to shoot when I cried out, "Rav Meir promised me I would finish Shas; I have to remain alive in order to do so!" Somehow, I survived, though the boys at my side were murdered.

After the war, I made my way to America, where the pervasive gashmiyus made me slowly lose all connection to Yiddishkeit. I married a nice Jewish girl who wasn't religious. By that point, neither was I. We had children and made a beautiful life for ourselves, but religion had no part in it.

Then one night, I had a startling dream, in which Rav Meir appeared to me. I recognized him immediately, but wondered: Why had he come? He began to speak, and he sounded upset. He had taanos on me. "You're alive only because you pledged to finish Shas, and I advocated on your behalf. Now get out of bed and go learn!"

It was as if he were standing right next to me. I couldn't go back to sleep and the dream troubled me greatly. I began to think about the life I had left behind, about my family, about sitting on Rav Meir's shoulders. And I vividly remembered the cry when I called out from the threshold of death. It was all so fresh, as though it happened yesterday.

Without question, the time had come to change my ways, to return to the ways of old, to begin learning Shas. I called my children together and told them everything: about my past life, about my promise. I also told them about the dream and Rav Meir's demand that I fulfill my pledge.

We were all so inspired. Not only did I completely turn my life around, but my children and their families did, too.

"Today," concluded the old man, "I am celebrating that *siyum*."

Rav Meir had a dream.

His children, the lomdei haDaf, have dreams.

How beautiful it is when those dreams are one and the same.

Worthy Investment

EARLY ONE MORNING, YERUCHEM, A SENIOR *AVREICH* living in Ramat Aharon in Bnei Brak, was davening in the local "*shtieblach*"(*minyan* factory). It was Chol HaMoed and with all the *simchas beis hasho'eivah* celebrations going on in the neighborhood each night, most of the town's inhabitants had gone to sleep late the night before. For the most part, Bnei Brak was not up and running at 6:00 in the morning, and the shuls were very quiet. Though in two hours the *shtieblach* would be a hub of busyness, for now there were barely twelve people in attendance at the first *minyan*.

Nevertheless, as is the custom, as soon as the Torah was removed from the *aron*, the *gabbai* called out, "Kohen!10 shekel!" with the normal starting price for bidding for the honor. However, with almost no one in attendance, that's where the price remained. Yeruchem felt this was a disgrace for the Sefer Torah. No one was bidding on it? So he called out, "15 shekel!"

It wasn't much but it was something. Yeruchem didn't really have any extra money. A *yungerman* who had been in kollel for many years, he was struggling just to make ends meet. With all of the Yom Tov expenses, he was down to a few shekels in his bank account. And with a wedding coming up, he had to find a way to come up with 100,000 shekel. But the *kavod* of the Torah was important to him.

The bidding ended the moment it started, and the *gabbai* began to sell the next *aliyah* and all the rest of the requisite *aliyos* for Chol HaMoed. With each initial opening bid of 10 shekel, Yeruchem hiked it up by 5 shekel every time. It was his small contribution to the greater *kvod haTorah*.

When the time came to call up the people for *aliyos*, there wasn't much of a choice; there were so few people in attendance. However, standing in the back was an elderly, *chashuve*-looking individual, someone Yeruchem had not seen before, and he told the *gabbai* to give the man an *aliyah*.

After davening, the prestigious-looking man approached Yeruchem and thanked him for the *aliyah*. "Do I know you?"

Yeruchem responded that as far as he could recall, the two of them had never met.

"Then may I ask why you were *mechabed* me with the *aliyah*?"

Yeruchem confessed that the man had a *chashuv* appearance, so he wanted to give him a *kibbud*.

At first, the guest was silent. He seemed moved. Finally, he spoke. "I want to tell you something. I am, *baruch Hashem,* a person of means. I came from London for Yom Tov and pretty much everywhere I go, people honor me for my money. But you had no idea; you are the first person I can remember who did not honor me solely because of my money.

"I'd like to be *makir tov*. Tell me what I can do for you."

The entire conversation took Yeruchem by surprise. He wasn't looking for charity and had no intentions of receiving a kickback for his gesture. He thanked the fellow for his generosity but declined the offer. However, the grateful Yid was not so easily put off. "Please tell me of an upcoming expense."

This was very embarrassing, yet clearly the wealthy man wanted to do something. Finally, Yeruchem relented. "We are making a *chasunah* for our daughter in a few weeks." The wealthy man asked him to come to the apartment where he was staying. He sat Yeruchem down and pulled out a checkbook, wrote a check, and handed it to Yeruchem. The check was for 100,000 shekel (about $30,000).

Yeruchem, a struggling yungerman, pushed himself to pay for four aliyos. He wanted to display an extra dose of kvod haTorah.

That small investment paid off with a dividend of 100,000 shekel.

There's no investment quite like kvod haTorah.

Blood, Sweat, and Torah

IN 1940, WHEN REUVEN FAIN (LATER ROSH YESHIVAH OF Yeshiva Torah Vodaath) was 16 years old, he and the rest of Yeshivas Mir traveled across Europe and part of Asia, eventually making their way to Shanghai, China, where they were safe from the Nazis. There they learned and lived with tremendous *mesirus nefesh*. After the war, when the yeshivah left Shanghai, the vast majority of the Jews left with them. But the mark they left on the Torah world during those years will never be forgotten.

Rav Reuven later described Shanghai as the biggest *cheder* in the world, where they learned the concept of *mesirus nefesh*. In the summer months, it was suffocatingly and stiflingly hot. At times, the temperatures reached 40° to 50°C (104° to 122°F). The oppressive heat drained people of their strength and sapped them of their energy. There were days in which the *bachurim* were so weak that they had no strength to walk to the *beis midrash* in the Beis Aharon Yeshivah, but hobbled there instead.

Due to the war, the local authorities dictated that at certain times all windows had to be shuttered and closed. And because of that, the homes became ovens, with the temperature reaching an unbearable 60° to 70°C (140° to 158°F)!

The sweat poured forth from their bodies, drenching the *talmidim's* clothing as if they'd bathed in them. The beads of sweat dripped down their foreheads, causing their eyes to burn. The droplets also fell onto the pages of the Gemara and soaked them. In order to prevent the perspiration from blurring the ink of the precious letters, the *bachurim* would take towels and cover the pages, so the only words exposed were the words they were learning.

Because the water was often contaminated, they had to boil it before drinking. But due to the excessive heat, the water never cooled off and it was difficult to drink the lukewarm water in order to keep hydrated. What's more, the terrifying sounds of explosions often disturbed their sleep.

Since the *bachurim's* accommodations were not right near the yeshivah building, and they were required to carry their papers on them at all times, they did not leave the yeshivah buildings on Friday nights, but slept right there.

Despite the difficult circumstances, the one thing they tried to do was learn Torah! And incredibly, despite insurmountable odds, they *shteiged*!

Rav Reuven described the *ahavas Torah* with passion and emotion; he spoke about the one "Rav Chaim" (*sefer* of Rav Chaim Soloveitchik of Brisk) to be found in Shanghai. Every person had his chance to learn from it for one night. "My turn came on Friday night," wrote Rav Reuven, "so instead of sleeping, I learned the famous Rav Chaim on '*mi'pi kesavam*' throughout the night; I used twenty-eight towels to soak up the sweat! I learned that Friday night from 6:00 in the evening until the rays of the sun rose the next morning. I never experienced anything sweeter."

When asked how he managed during those days to keep

learning despite the hardship and the worry about his family, Rav Reuven said, "It was Rav Chatzkel Levenstein, our mashgiach, who pulled us through."

Rav Chatzkel continued giving his powerful *shmuessen* during this era and often pointed out the differences between the European and Chinese cultures. In Europe, horses pulled wagons; in China, people did. Though one may have wondered how the Chinese people, who are mostly smaller than their European counterparts, had the strength to pull those rickshaws day in and day out, Rav Chatzkel highlighted that we have way more power and stamina than we think. It's just a matter of hard work and building up those capabilities.

With this in mind, Rav Chatzkel explained that when Chazal enjoin us in *Pirkei Avos* (5:23) to be bold as a leopard, light as an eagle, swift as a deer, and strong as a lion to carry out Hashem's will, they don't mean it as a *mashal.* Rather, a person has it within his capacity to actually make these characteristics part of himself. Just as the people in China used all their *kochos* to do their work, even to the point of harnessing the power of an animal, one should use all his powers to serve Hashem.

This is what the Mirrer *talmidim* managed to do in Shanghai in terms of *limud Torah,* thanks to Rav Chatzkel's encouragement.

***

Reuven was privileged to learn in Shanghai with the young Nachum Partzovitz. Their second *seder* could last until 3 a.m., with just one small break to daven Maariv! Whoever heard of such *hasmadah*?!

Reuven and Nachum once went three days without any food. When Rav Nachum was later asked how they survived, he had a one-word answer. A *Rashba*!

It is no wonder that this group developed into the builders of Torah for the next generation.

In a moving and poetic tribute to the *kedoshim* of the Holocaust in *Binyan Nachum*, Rav Nachum Partzovitz composed an ode to those who made it to Shanghai, but died there. They were buried in this foreign and unfamiliar territory, a land never trod upon by our ancestors. But they were not the only ones left behind. As Rav Nachum wrote, addressing the deceased:

"The final *levayah* we attended in Shanghai was for the wagonloads of *shaimos* from the hundreds of *sefarim* we learned together in the '*yamim noraim*' (he refers to all the time spent there as days of awe) of the Shanghai ghetto. The *shaimos*, drenched with tears and sweat, will serve as a *koras ruach,* a soothing balm, for your souls in Gan Eden..."

The toil and tears we invest in our learning and in our sefarim are not mere materialistic mementos; they are the lifeblood of our existence.

Unthinkable

RAV PINCHAS SCHREIBER, AN EXCEPTIONALLY FINE *talmid chacham* and *tzaddik*, lived with his wife and family in Yerushalayim. His wife left early each morning to go to work, and he took care of his children until 8:45, when he left to his kollel. At that time, Devorah, a kind and warm woman, came to take care of the children in their home.

Devorah and her husband had been married for 10 years and had not yet been blessed with children. It wasn't easy for a childless woman to take care of someone else's children. She often wondered when she would be able to take care of her own. But she continued to have faith that one day, she'd be blessed with a child of her own. In the meantime, she did her job with commitment, dedication, and exceptional care. It meant a lot to Devorah that thanks to her efforts, Rav Pinchas could learn without worry.

But then she was faced with an enormous challenge.

Until now, every time she and her husband had gone to doctors, the results were disappointing. One day, they were informed that a doctor in Tel Aviv was using experimental treatments and many couples had found their salvation through his efforts. Devorah called the doctor's office and asked for an appointment. The woman on the other end of the line was courteous and patient, tactfully asking questions and taking down the information. Before giving Devorah a date for an appointment, the receptionist told Devorah she would have to check the calendar. She put Devorah on hold for what seemed to be like an eternity. At long last, the receptionist came back on the phone and explained that the waiting list for an appointment was six months.

Six months?!

Devorah knew that many others wanted to see this doctor and it could take a while to get in, but she had never expected it to take this long. Though she begged and pleaded, she was unsuccessful.

She continued to diligently take care of the Schreiber children. Every day, she arrived at 8:45 and Rav Pinchas left to the *beis midrash,* but not before thanking Devorah for her sense of duty and the love she showed his children. He knew not to take her for granted.

Six months slowly passed.

On the day of the appointment, Devorah boarded an early morning bus to Tel Aviv. At 8:30, though, she suddenly remembered that she had forgotten to inform the Schreibers she would not be coming that day. By now, it was too late to find another babysitter. Devorah was faced with a dilemma. On the one hand, she didn't want to cause Rav Pinchas to miss his learning. For so long, she'd felt as if she had a *zechus* in his learning and now, albeit inadvertently, she would be causing *bittul Torah*; he would not be able to leave the house without a babysitter. On the other hand, after waiting for 10 years, she had waited an additional six months for this appointment. If she canceled now, she would most likely have to wait another six months.

After going back and forth, Devorah decided to do the unthinkable.

She was going to skip the appointment.

She alighted at the next bus stop, crossed the street, took a bus back to her neighborhood, and walked into the Schreiber home at 8:45 without saying a word. As he did every day, Rav Pinchas thanked her and walked out the door. He had no idea what his loyal babysitter had just given up.

Over the next two hours, Devorah took care of the children and held herself together. However, when they went in for a nap, she sat down on the couch, opened a *Tehillim,* and cried with great emotion, as 10 years of pain and frustration burst out. She davened to Hashem and begged for a child of her own, asking that the *zechus* of her *mesirus nefesh* for Torah should stand by her. Her *Tehillim* soaked up her tears until she could cry no longer.

As the children continued to sleep, Devorah picked up the phone and called the doctor. She apologized for missing her appointment, explaining that something unexpected had come up, and asked to reschedule. The receptionist was very understanding. She said she would take care of rescheduling and put Devorah on hold. This time, Devorah knew what was coming when the woman came back on the line: an availability in six months. The receptionist assured Devorah that if someone canceled, she would be the first to receive a call. But Devorah knew people generally didn't cancel appointments with this doctor. Except her, that is.

She booked the appointment, expecting to wait another six months.

She never made it to the appointment.

A few weeks later, Devorah discovered that she was expecting a child. Eight months later, she and her husband were blessed with a son.

That would be their only child.

Today, he lives in Yerushalayim, a talmid chacham with a wonderful family of his own.

Very possibly in the merit of a childless woman who displayed indescribable sacrifice for limud Torah.

A Worthwhile Wait

THOUGH BORN IN AMERICA, RAV SHLOMO BREVDA TRAVeled to Yerushalayim in order to learn by the Brisker Rav, Rav Yitzchak Zev Soloveitchik. During that period, he also developed a relationship with the Chazon Ish, Rav Avraham Yeshayah Karelitz, who lived in Bnei Brak.

Ezra, a *bachur* from Yerushalayim, was badly hurt by shrapnel during the Israeli War of Independence in 1948. For months after, Ezra lay in the hospital. Even once he was released, he was readmitted multiple times for extensive surgeries to repair all the damage he had sustained. Following every operation, he had to recuperate for a while and then undergo rehabilitation in the hospital, where he was exposed to the depraved values of the secular world, each time causing him to slip more in his spirituality.

But Ezra was a *gibbor* (man of strength) and despite all he was enduring, he told his parents of his desire to attend *yeshivah gedolah.* And he did. Although it was not easy, he persevered and overcame tremendous obstacles. Ezra was on fire.

One day in the early 1950s, Ezra visited his doctor and

complained of persistent pain. His doctor informed him that he must undergo yet another operation; otherwise he could not expect to live pain-free. But this time, Ezra protested. He had worked so hard to get to where he was in his *ruchniyus* and wasn't interested in slipping down the ladder on account of the less than optimal environment in the hospital.

His parents didn't know what to do. He was still not fully recovered and walked with a serious limp. They knew that if he did not undergo the operation, he would continue to suffer. The question was: Should he undergo the operation and relieve his physical pain? Or should he not undergo the operation and keep his soul from becoming exposed to the *tumah* of the secular world?

Shlomo Brevda, still a young man, met up with Ezra at that time. Hearing from him and his parents about his dilemma, Shlomo offered to take Ezra to seek counsel from the Chazon Ish. Though he was already very old and weak, the Chazon Ish could still be counted on for advice and encouragement. He would be able to guide Ezra.

Shlomo and Ezra traveled to Bnei Brak. When they came close to the house of the Chazon Ish, Shlomo told Ezra that despite the Chazon Ish's awe-inspiring greatness, there was no reason to be afraid. But Ezra reminded Shlomo that he had spoken to many rabbanim in his life, and if there was nothing to be frightened of then, there was nothing to fear now. When Shlomo emphasized the point once more — that there was no reason to fear meeting the Chazon Ish — Ezra became frustrated, reiterating that he would not be fearful. Not wanting to cause the boy further agitation, Shlomo let the matter rest.

When they finally arrived at the house, it was already dark outside, and the house itself was dimly lit. When Shlomo and Ezra knocked on the door, they were allowed entry only on condition that they say nothing to the Chazon Ish, who was extremely weak, and only give him the name of the person who needs a *yeshuah*. After receiving a *berachah,* they were to leave immediately. The

Chazon Ish's attendants didn't want to cause him any added stress. These restrictions did not stop people from coming to the *gadol,* however. Although they realized his time was limited, those in need of salvation yearned for his blessing.

At this stage, the Chazon Ish could hardly move; his bed had been moved to the small porch. Shlomo first entered by himself. There was only a small amount of light shining on the *gadol's* face. Yet even in his compromised state, he exuded holiness and a special glow.

As soon as the Chazon Ish noticed Shlomo, he started asking him questions about his learning and how many *blatt* he had learned recently and the name of his *chavrusa.* Shlomo tried to redirect the conversation toward the main purpose of his visit, Ezra, but the Chazon Ish asked one question after another, all unconnected to Ezra and his need for a blessing.

Finally, Shlomo was able to get to the point of his visit. However, seeing that the Chazon Ish was able to speak, he began to discuss Ezra's situation in detail. The Chazon Ish asked if he'd brought along the young man and requested that he be brought into the room.

When the Chazon Ish asked the young man questions — What did the doctors say? Could the surgery wait? If he didn't have the surgery, would this cause only pain or irreversible damage? — Ezra gave no response. Although he'd been so sure he would not be afraid, he seemed petrified, unable to get a word out. Shlomo held his hand and reassured him. He told him not to be fearful, but as hard as he tried, the boy wasn't able to utter a single word. The Chazon Ish also tried reassuring him but his efforts were futile, as well. Finally, after much persuasion, Ezra was able to utter a response and explained that without surgery, no further damage would come about, but he would remain in pain.

The Chazon Ish suddenly sat up in his bed with newfound vigor and strength. He reached out and enthusiastically grabbed hold of the Ezra's hands with both of his, gazed deeply into his eyes, and slowly enunciated four words, "*Atah... rotzeh... lilmod... Torah...* — You... want... to... learn... Torah!" And he advised him to wait six months and then revisit the situation.

Ezra thanked the *gadol hador* and returned to yeshivah, imbued with admiration for the Chazon Ish. What greater *chizuk* could there be?

But he never had his chance to revisit the situation with the Chazon Ish.

Ten days later, the *gadol hador* was gone.

Thousands followed his *mitah* to its final resting place. Among them limped and cried a young man, who now had the *ahavas haTorah* and the validation the Chazon Ish had seared into his very being.

The Priest's Point

RAV YOSEF SHLOMO KAHANEMAN, THE PONOVEZHER Rav, made it a point to attend every *siyum* he could. It didn't make a difference how big or how small, he was there. Even when a *baal habayis* finished *Chayei Adam* or *Ein Yaakov*, he would come and he would speak. He marveled at how a layman could spend so many years working to finish the entire *sefer*.

Before the war, when he still lived in the city of Ponovezh, there was a huge Siyum HaShas in the city. Everyone was involved in some way, preparing to do their part to enhance the *simchah*. The community was in a frenzy; it looked like they were setting up for a royal wedding.

The local priest took note of the tumult and asked the Ponovezher Rav what was going on. The Rav and the priest, an intelligent individual, enjoyed a cordial relationship. Since the priest had connections with the authorities, the Rav wanted to make sure he was on good terms with the Jewish community.

Now the Rav explained that the people were celebrating a *siyum* on all of Shas. Eager to understand, the priest pressed the Rav to better try and appreciate why this was such an accomplishment. "Tell me, what is the Talmud?"

Seeing that the priest was genuinely interested, the Rav invited him to his home, led him to his bookcase, and showed him his set of Vilna Shas. All twenty volumes.

The priest was bewildered. "This is it? This is what the entire commotion is about? Just a few volumes? What for?" Unimpressed, he thanked the Rav for his time and left his home.

The *siyum* took place a few days later; it was a grand event, a sight to behold. At the *siyum*, the Rav spoke to the entire *kehillah,* recounted the story with the priest, and asked the assembled, "What should I have answered him? There is no way for him to understand that every *Rishon* and *Acharon*, all *meforshim* and *poskim*, and every *lomdishe chakirah* is based on these twenty 'small' volumes. Thousands upon thousands of volumes, filling so, so many *sefarim shranks,* are based on these twenty volumes of Shas. How could this non-Jew possibly understand that the entirety of *Torah She'be'al Peh*, our Oral Law, is contained within these sacred and hallowed tomes? There is no way he could comprehend!

"But, on the other hand, *Rabbosai, der galach iz gerecht*! The priest is right! Sitting here before me are tens of Yidden from our city who have finished all of Shas. So it must be that Shas is not impossible to finish. It's not all that big; it's possible for everyone to achieve!"

Rav Shimon Hershler added: Hashem says to Bnei Yisrael that the Torah is close to us, right there in our mouths to learn and to keep (Devarim 30:14):

כי קרוב אליך הדבר **מאד** **בפיך** **ובלבבך** **לעשתו** . *The roshei teivos of the last four words of the pasuk spell* מבול*. This is* *a hint that even in our inferior world, a storm of confusion, where we are flooded and deluged with heresy and falsehood, the Torah is right there for us.*

We can learn, we can accomplish.

The Torah is accessible to us.

Take it from a priest.

The Story Behind the Prize

IN 1970, WHEN CHACHAM OVADIAH YOSEF WAS 50 YEARS old, he was awarded the prestigious Israel Prize for Torah Literature for his *sefarim* titled *Yabia Omer*, a collection of halachic responsa, which were rightfully touted as a wondrous achievement in the world of Torah. Accompanying the prize was a generous cash gift. At the award ceremony, he made a *kiddush Hashem* when he refused to shake the hands of the prime minister, Golda Meir. But there is another story connected to the prize, one not as well-known, which conveys the importance accorded by *gedolim* to the Torah learning of any Jew.

When Chacham Ovadiah was already older, Reb David Yifrach asked him a bold question. "How were you *zocheh* to become such a phenomenal *marbitz Torah*?"

"Six people became 600,000," was the cryptic response.

Seeing the puzzled look on Reb David's face, Chacham Ovadiah smiled and revealed his secret.

As you know, years ago I was the recipient of the Israeli Prize. The award ceremony was scheduled for the Israeli Day of Independence. Other prizes were awarded that day, for achievements in science, music, and medicine. The award presentation was scheduled for 7:00 p.m., and the representative told me to be there early.

The timing presented a problem, however, because every day from 6:00 until 7:00, I gave a shiur to six fine Jews who came straight from work to the Beis Yisrael shul. This shiur was very dear to me; these working men sacrificed tremendously to attend every day, and I saw their love and desire for Torah on a constant basis. Since I had begun giving the class, I had never missed. I was not going to miss now, even if it meant relinquishing the award and a large amount of money, money that could certainly be put to good use.

The "big day" arrived. I came to give my shiur at the regular time and refused to allow the attendees to feel rushed in any way. As I always did, I explained each point, breaking each one down so that everyone could understand. As usual, the shiur ran for one hour, from 6:00 until 7:00. When it was over at 7:00 and I was getting ready to leave, the representative who had spoken to me earlier arrived and snapped at me, "Why didn't you come yet? The dignitaries have already arrived. It's really not nice to make them wait."

I could not tolerate the insult to the honor of the Torah, the way he degraded limud Torah be'rabbim, so I countered, "Not only did I end the shiur at 7:00 so as not to waste a moment of Torah learning, but now I am going to daven with the members of my beloved shiur." After davening, I finally left, and my dear talmidim from the shiur made their way over to the ceremony, as well.

I arrived at the event at 7:30, 30 minutes late. When I walked in, the organizer, clearly agitated, threw the envelope at me. "Take it!" Though I really needed the money, I refused to accept the envelope. I could not remain indifferent to the way the coordinators had disparaged those who learn Torah.

However, I told the organizer that I still intended to speak.

He introduced me and I made my way up to the podium. In front of the huge crowd, I spoke with authority. "Standing here before us we have the prime minister and the president and quite a large audience. But there are six individuals here today who are more prominent than any of you. Because they learn Torah — and that is more chashuv than this entire event!"

As I spoke, I could see the president, Zalman Shazar, who grew up in Mir, Poland, and came from a prominent Lubavitch family, nodding his head in agreement. As a descendant of the Bach, Rav Yoel Sirkis, he knew the truth. He understood that Torah learning superseded any such gathering, and the message touched him deeply. After I finished speaking, the president came over to me and asked me to please accept the envelope. Only when I saw that my message had been received did I agree.

Chacham Ovadiah concluded his story and punctuated, "It is all *siyata d'Shmaya*, but if I had to point to one incident, I believe it is because of my *mesirus nefesh* for those six men that today 600,000 people listen to my voice."

What is more, those six working men merited children who became Torah giants in their own right.

Such is the power of sincere Torah learning.

Returning the Favor

Anyone who has taught for more than a year or two has most likely encountered some classes that are very difficult to teach. Of course, they're made up of wonderful children, but school — and sitting in a classroom for hours on end — is simply not their thing.

ONE YEAR, RABBI NOSSON BUCHFELD, A SEVENTH-grade rebbi, had his hands full with one such class. In previous years, he had rarely thrown a student out of class, but had always found a way to work with each one. With this year's tough class, however, not kicking anyone out of class seemed like an impossibility. From the moment they entered the classroom, the boys made noise, and every day a few of them had to be asked to leave. After that, the rest of the class usually calmed down, but it was certainly a less than ideal learning atmosphere.

Among the challenging students, Dovid took the prize. Dovid didn't seem to communicate well. He had trouble making eye contact; he kind of looked past the person addressing him. Even more problematic, he was loud and boisterous. Even when his teachers told him to sit down and keep quiet, he refused to listen, turning confrontational and stirring up trouble.

Reb Nosson spoke to Dovid's parents, who couldn't offer much in the way of solutions. They admitted to struggling with similar outbursts and in fact, Dovid had been living with his uncle and aunt, Dr. and Mrs. Glassman, for the past few months. At home, it was just too difficult.

While Rabbi Buchfeld felt somewhat validated that this issue was not only a school issue and was certainly not his fault, he was no closer to solving the problem. As the months of the school year passed, the situation deteriorated. Dovid was slipping away. It became more and more demanding to have him in the classroom. Finally, the school year ended. Rabbi Buchfeld had survived.

Barely.

As for Dovid, that was only the beginning of a trying journey. Soon after his stint in Rabbi Buchfeld's class, he flitted from one yeshivah to the next. In time, he was spiraling down a long, dark, black hole, with questionable company, and recreational activities equally detrimental and dangerous to his well-being. By the time he was 18, on many days he himself didn't know where he was. Occasionally, Rabbi Buchfeld would pass him on the street and try to make conversation with him. Most often, he got nowhere. It's not that Dovid was upset with his rebbi, it's just that that was not where his mind was.

More years passed. It seemed like Dovid was lost.

Then something changed.

Slowly, there were improvements. Dovid was holding down a job, a major breakthrough. In addition, Rabbi Buchfeld would walk into the bagel shop where Dovid was employed and he was able to engage him in conversation, a conversation that actually went somewhere, with Dovid interjecting a few "*baruch Hashem's*" along the way.

Rabbi Buchfeld was happy for his former *talmid*. He knew he had had such a rough go of it, and he hoped he was starting to find his way. Then one day, Dovid left his job and Rabbi Buchfeld stopped seeing him around. He wasn't sure what had happened to him, but assumed he'd simply moved.

And he hoped for the best.

One Friday night, Rabbi Buchfeld was getting ready for davening when Dovid's uncle, Dr. Glassman, called him aside and asked if he could speak to him outside the shul. *Kabbalas Shabbos* was just beginning and generally, Rabbi Buchfeld didn't like to speak about school matters on Shabbos. But Dr. Glassman seemed to feel it was important and claimed it would only take a minute.

They stepped outside into the hallway and Dr. Glassman began, "About 10 years ago, Dovid was in your class and though it wasn't easy, you put your heart and soul into trying to reach him. I thought you would be happy to know that he just became a *chassan*."

Rabbi Buchfeld was very pleased to hear the news, but was also curious as to where Dovid was holding in life. He hadn't heard anything for two years now. A broad smile spread across Dovid's uncle's face in answer to Rabbi Buchfeld's question. "You don't know? Dovid sits and learns *yomam va'lailah*, day and night! He has completely turned his life around. You wouldn't believe it. It's *mamash* a *neis*!"

Rabbi Buchfeld felt like he was going to cry. How could Dovid have made such an about-face? He and Dr. Glassman spoke a little more and Rabbi Buchfeld discovered that Dovid was learning with *chashuve talmidei chachamim* and didn't waste a moment of his day, and his *kallah* came from a beautiful, *Torahdik* family. Rabbi Buchfeld thanked Dr. Glassman for sharing the news and continued to shake his head in disbelief.

And he kept wondering. How did this happen?

But then he was reminded of a massive fire that had taken place several years earlier, which had destroyed a yeshivah for struggling youth. When the firemen came, they hurried everyone out of the building. Though everyone was safe and the firemen had already announced that nobody may enter the building, one of the boys realized that the Sefer Torah was still inside, and he pushed past the firemen. Risking his life, he ran into the building as it filled with smoke, made his way to the *aron kodesh,* and courageously carried the Sefer Torah to safety.

That boy was Dovid!

Of course, Dovid received a tremendous amount of assistance and support along his way back home, from family and friends and rebbeim and strangers. Additionally, so many individuals davened for his yeshuah through the years. But perhaps something else also contributed to his dramatic turnaround.

Here was a boy who was far removed from Torah for so long. But there was still a spark inside of him, and that spark inspired him to save the Sefer Torah at all costs.

The Torah is Toras chaim.

It's alive.

Perhaps when one sacrifices himself for the Torah, the Torah itself pulls him away from the dangers that threaten his life.

Dovid saved the Torah — and the Torah saved him.

We Will Live On!

The following vignettes are proof of the eternal connection between the Jewish people, Hashem, and His Torah.

THE PONOVEZHER RAV, RAV YOSEF SHLOMO KAHANEMAN, exhibited seemingly endless strength. Even while the world he knew was being destroyed, he had already begun to rebuild. The ever-flourishing *ihr haTorah*, the Torah city of Bnei Brak, is a testament to his efforts.

As a champion of Torah, Rav Kahaneman traveled the world, collecting funds to support the institutions he built. Even as he got on in years, his relentless nature allowed him no rest. He continued his travels, traipsing from one city to the next and then onto the next country. Often, he arrived home a day before Yom Tov.

One Succos, a young Eliezer Turk and his father, who lived near the Ponovezher Rav, came to visit as they did every Yom Tov. The year was 1968, and the Rav was 82 years old, an age when most people spend the bulk of their time relaxing. But the entire concept of relaxation was foreign to the Rav. He couldn't bring himself to slow down.

As soon as the Turks arrived, they were greeted by the rebbetzin, who motioned that today they would not be able to visit the Rav. She explained in hushed tones that over the last few weeks, the Rav had traveled overseas, arriving home only on Erev Succos. Even so, she told them, as soon as he came into the house, he didn't waste any time. He got dressed for Yom Tov and headed out to his beloved yeshivah, Yeshivas Ponovezh. After Maariv, only after greeting everyone, each individual with a personal *gut Yom Tov,* had he returned home. Despite his exhaustion, he did not rush the *seudah*, instead relishing every moment in the *succah*. Even afterward, he didn't lie down in the cot in the *succah,* but sat down to learn, expecting to go into bed when sleep overtook him. But that never happened.

He learned the entire night.

When morning came, the Rav davened in the yeshivah and then made his way back to the *succah* for the *seudah,* again celebrating the Yom Tov with fervor and joy. Nothing was rushed. On the contrary, the meal may have taken longer than usual.

After the rebbetzin finished her tale about her husband, she explained to the amazed father and son that it would not be possible to visit him now. Of course, they understood. It is physically impossible for a person to go without sleep, so they expected the Rav to finally catch some shuteye; they didn't want to interrupt even for a quick *shalom aleichem.*

Invigorated with the firsthand account of a tireless *gadol,* Eliezer and his father turned to leave. Before leaving, they watched as the rebbetzin went to check on the Rav, peeking out the window to the *succah.*

Sure enough, he was fine — sitting at a *shtender,* learning with insatiable hunger!

He had been away so long, he had to rest up.

And he was doing it the only way he knew how.

***

Rebbetzin Rochel Weiss was the wife of Rav Shabsi Weiss of the Givat Shaul community and the mother of a large *mishpachah,* the oldest of whom was merely 15. When Rebbetzin Weiss, who was beloved by so many, was diagnosed with a serious illness, word of her condition quickly spread and hundreds davened for her recovery. In every corner of Givat Shaul, *Tehillim* groups were formed; it was common to find clusters of women walking back and forth to shul at night to recite *Tehillim.*

Despite the prayers, the rebbetzin passed away, and a tangible sadness filled the air in Givat Shaul. A lengthy procession followed her *mitah* to the Har Tamir section of Har HaMenuchos where she would be buried, one of the first in the new section of the ancient mountain.

It had been a very long day and the sun was beginning to set. Rebbetzin Rochel's father, Rav Moshe Shimon, stood at a fence that separated his daughter's burial plot from the main path. As a Kohen, he was unable to walk any farther, and his *talmidim* and others gathered around him. Mostly wrapped in silence, every so often Rav Moshe Shimon would interject an urgent "Are they finished?" On the surface, it was a question from a grieving father prevented by halachah from coming any closer to the gravesite. But there was more to it.

After a while, there was a loud proclamation that the grave had been covered. At that moment, another declaration could be heard, this time from Rav Moshe Shimon.

"Baruch Atah Hashem Elokeinu Melech ha'olam asher kideshanu be'mitzvosav ve'tzivanu la'asok be'divrei Sorah — Blessed are You, Hashem, King of the universe, Who has sanctified us with His commandments and has commanded us to engross ourselves in the words of Torah!"

He had just lost his beloved daughter. Yet the mourning father had the self-control and presence of mind to worry about *Birchos HaTorah* (which he could not recite as long as he was an *onein*, someone who has lost a close relative who has not yet been buried).

He reached the words, "May we and our offspring and the offspring of our offspring and the offspring of Your people... know Your Name and study Your Torah for its sake..." And the hearts of the listeners surrounding him began to shudder, as they watched a father returning a *pikadon,* a pledge, in full.

Perhaps those words held reassurance, as well.

A loving mother, devoted wife, and treasured daughter had been taken. Rav Moshe Shimon, however, was flanked by generations who would carry on the legacy.

Through Torah, the Jewish people live on.

***

Years ago, a man wanted to get his grandson into Yeshivas Ponovezh. He wrote a letter to Rav Berel Povarsky, to ask him to pull strings with his father, Rav Dovid, who was rosh yeshivah at the time, and was also acquainted with this man. Along with his request, the man included a *vort*:

In *Parashas Shemos,* Hashem commanded Aharon to go and greet his brother, Moshe; Aharon went out to meet Moshe and he kissed him. The Sforno (4:27) adds a small but very powerful idea: When Aharon kissed Moshe, he did so as one would kiss a *davar kadosh*, a holy item.

The grandfather writing the letter added his own interpretation to Sforno's: Though Aharon had not seen Moshe for many years, he didn't kiss him because he was his long-lost brother. Nor did he kiss him to congratulate him on being appointed leader of the Jewish people. Rather, he kissed him for one reason and one reason only. Just as one kisses a Sefer Torah when he sees it, when he saw Moshe, a living Sefer Torah, Aharon forgot all his other emotions and kissed him as one kisses a holy object.

The grandfather ended his letter, "This is a thought I had and I wanted to share it with you."

Rav Berel went to his father and told him, "An acquaintance of yours from years back wrote me a letter; he wants you to accept his grandson into the yeshivah."

Rav Dovid listened to the request but responded, "Even though I know the man from years back, that's not a reason to accept his grandson. You know I don't operate with *protektzia*."

Rav Berel countered, "But Abba, he shared a beautiful *derher* (insight) in a Sforno," and he repeated the sentiment about the love Aharon had for a living Sefer Torah.

Upon hearing the *vort,* Rav Dovid's eyes lit up and he excitedly responded, "Write back that we will accept his grandchild in the yeshivah. A man with such feelings for Yiddishkeit and Torah — we need to have his grandchildren in our yeshivah!"

For it's our love and devotion to Torah that keeps us connected.

***

Before agreeing to serve as *mesader kiddushin* at a *talmid's* wedding, Rav Chaim Stein, rosh yeshivah of Yeshivas Telshe in Cleveland, always asked the *talmid* to accept upon himself to learn an hour a day for the rest of his life. If an hour was not possible, Rav Chaim stated, then at least a half-hour. This hour/half-hour was sacred in Telshe; nothing and no one could get in the way of this most treasured period of the day.

During the last few days of his life, Rav Eliyahu Meir Bloch, one of Rav Chaim's predecessors as rosh yeshivah in Telshe, was bedridden in the hospital. Nearly incapacitated, Rav Elya Meir was hooked up to all types of machines to help keep him alive.

Suddenly, he pointed agitatedly to his mouth. He desperately wanted to say something. After struggling, he managed to say one word.

"*Lernen.*"

The *bachur* sitting at his bedside pulled out a Chumash and read aloud the *pesukim* with Rashi. After 30 minutes, the rosh yeshivah was completely depleted and whispered in a hoarse voice, "*Genug.* Enough."

A few hours later, the routine repeated itself. The rosh yeshivah mustered his strength to request "*lernen*" and listened as his *talmid* read aloud from the Chumash.

When the half-hour ended, Rav Elya Meir smiled and stated, "*Genug.*"

He had done it. Another hour of learning on an exceedingly difficult day.

Decades earlier, he had been mekabel upon himself to learn at least an hour a day. On the run, away from a family he would never see again, Rav Elya Meir desired to be tethered to Torah. Come what may.

And he continued.

Up until the very end.

***

A man once visited Rav Elazar Menachem Man Shach to request a *berachah.* The man, a *talmid chacham* in his own right, had been the *chavrusa* of Rav Shach many years earlier in Slutzk, when Rav Leizer Shach was still Leizer Shach. After receiving the sage's blessing, the *talmid chacham* walked out of the room and burst into tears. When asked why, he explained: I'm going to tell you why he became Rav Shach — and I didn't:

> *When Leizer and I learned be'chavrusa, we were so poor, we had nothing to eat. Furthermore, we were shivering in the cold beis midrash, without any wood to heat the room. But we were learning. And learning.*
>
> *I said to Leizer, "If you could ask the Ribbono Shel Olam for one thing, what would it be? I'll tell you what my bakashah would be. Of course, I want to learn Torah mi'toch hadchak, under extreme circumstances. But just a little less poverty — a bit more food, a bit more warmth. That's all I need."*
>
> *But you know what Leizer would have asked for? This is what he said to me: "Lernen, lernen, un noch lernen. Learning, learning, and more learning!" That's all he wanted, and look where he is now.*

"So tell me," he stated. "Should I not cry?"

Rav Shach hungered only for more and more Torah: "*Lo ra'av la'lechem ve'lo tzama la'mayim ki im lishmoa eis divrei Hashem —* Not a hunger for bread nor a thirst for water, but to hear the words of Hashem" (*Amos* 8:11).

With such aspirations for Torah, the Jewish nation will certainly live on!

TEFILLAH

Anytime Anyplace

Rav Yitzchak Tuvia Weiss, the Gaavad of Yerushalayim, has recounted many episodes that had occurred during his life. These memorable events were compiled in a collection of zichronos, Rabbeinu HaGadol Amro. The following is his recollection of his escape from his hometown and some of the ensuing events.

IN THE CITY OF PEZINOK, SLOVAKIA, WHERE YITZCHAK grew up, there was a tradition that 500 years earlier, eighty holy souls had been burned alive, among them the *av beis din* of the city. As a remembrance, a wooden tablet stood at the entranceway to the shul. Etched into the woodwork were the names of all of the *kedoshim,* along with the prayer of *Keil Malei Rachamim,* flanked by two large flames signifying the manner in which they were killed. Whenever *Yizkor* was recited in shul, these names were read aloud.

Until the community met its tragic end.

The Nazis stormed into the town on the fifth day of *Parashas Acharei Mos*, 5699/1939. Since the war had not yet begun, the community was unprepared for the horror and trauma, but they were to learn soon enough. On Shabbos, after the Nazis had already made their presence felt, they turned their attention to the shul, searching for a *korban*. However, by the time they entered the shul at midday, everyone had already gone home. Thus, they entered the Weiss home, which was right near the shul.

The German guards grabbed Yitzchak's father, Reb Shlomo Weiss, and pointed a gun at him. After roughing him up, they brought him to the synagogue and demanded that he translate everything written on the memorial tablet. He did as he was told, calmly explaining that the martyrs had been burned alive. Not to be outdone, the Nazis bragged, "We are not going to burn you. Instead, we will shoot you right here and right now." Only thanks to his wife's frantic pleas did they agree to spare Reb Shlomo's life.

But the shul would not be spared; the Nazis set it ablaze. Surprisingly, though, they gave permission to remove the Sifrei Torah before they began. Twenty holy scrolls were taken out and brought into the Weiss home. But the Nazis had more on their agenda. They forced the rav of the town, Rav Yehoshua Leib Shillel, and other rabbanim to remove the benches and tables from the shul and set them ablaze. As the rabbanim did so, the Nazis rained down a brutal beating on each of the men, and they shamed them and ripped at their beards. Rav Yehoshua Leib survived the incident but knew he must stay out of the limelight and tend to the *kehillah's* needs behind closed doors. Reb Shlomo Weiss took over the Shabbos *derashos* and continued to inspire the terrified congregation, infusing them with hope and faith.

Sunday morning prior to daybreak, the community members sent a special messenger, 12-year-old Yitzchak Weiss, to nearby Pressburg (Bratislava) to inform the heads of the *kehillah* of what had transpired in their town, and to ask for help. In the eyes of the community, Yitzchak, who was just a child, had a better chance of making it to Pressburg than an adult. Arriving in Pressburg, Yitzchak entered the special chamber where the key members of the community met, informed them of the atrocities the Nazis had committed, and relayed the message requesting assistance.

The head of the committee, Rav Schwartz, explained that nothing could stand in the way of the Nazi hatred, and they, too, were helpless against it. However, he informed Yitzchak that Rav Solomon Schoenfeld and Rav Michael Ber Weissmandl had arranged a Kindertransport of ten children that would travel to London, England, to escape the Nazis. Nine children from Pressburg had already signed up. If Yitzchak wanted, he could become the tenth. They instructed him to go immediately to the *vaad hakehillah* and register for the last spot. Which is exactly what he did.

(As an aside, in a chance encounter 60 years later, Rav Yitzchak Tuvia met a Yid from Canada, Rav Shimon Werner, who told him that the tenth spot had originally been reserved for him. At the last moment, however, his mother changed her mind and didn't let him go. Thus, there was room for one more. Rav Yitzchak shared this story to emphasize how every Yid has his own path to salvation, as young Shimon made it out some other way.)

Now that Yitzchak was signed up for the transport, he returned to his hometown to prepare for his trip. On his final Shabbos, his shul gave him the *aliyah* for *maftir* so he could celebrate, to some extent, his upcoming bar mitzvah along with his family.

Before he knew it, the time had come to say goodbye. Overwhelmed with emotion, Yitzchak davened his final Maariv in the shul and cried to the Al-mighty. As he said goodbye to his mother, the tears came on their own. Saying goodbye is never easy, certainly not for someone who fears he may never see his parents again.

Yitzchak was set to travel from Pressburg, so he and his father made their way to the train station. As the two sat together on a bench, waiting for the train's arrival, Reb Shlomo pulled out a goodbye gift. He handed it to his son. It was a *siddur,* with a very short inscription:

"Daven to Hashem and you will find Him: *immer un umetum,* always and everywhere."

A while later, Yitzchak arrived in London. Although initially he was placed in an institution not conducive to his growth as a Yid, he was transferred soon after to a Sassover *mosad,* where he felt much more at home. Although this *mosad* was under the government auspices, it was certainly more in line with Torah *hashkafah*. However, his peace of mind would not last long. Because World War II had now become a reality and London was under siege, the British sent one million children from London to the villages surrounding the city.

Yitzchak was sent with four younger boys to Ely, a small village outside London, on a Friday. After greeting them warmly, their non-Jewish hosts told the boys they could rest and remove their hats. The children explained that as Jews, they always covered their heads. The non-Jews had never heard of such a thing; they had never seen Jews before. The boys also declined all food except for bread, fruit, and tea without milk. Once Shabbos arrived, even tea was off limits. Though other Jews, in the name of *pikuach nefesh,* tried to convince Yitzchak and his friends to give in, he held firm; he even delivered a penetrating "*derashah*," imploring his young companions not to be influenced, but to hold steadfast and be strong. You see, it was the week of his bar mitzvah. And although it was not the *derashah* he had anticipated, this became his bar mitzvah speech!

Soon after, thanks to the efforts of the Sassover Rebbe, Yitzchak was moved to new quarters, where he could live as a Jew. Yet he and the others were forced to go to a Jewish secular school for refugee children, where they were exposed to material not in line with their religious upbringing. Ultimately, Rav Shlomo Shapiro and his wife moved in with the boys and helped take care of them, though it was still not home. Somehow, Yitzchak also managed to watch the milking process at a nearby farm, making the milk he drank *chalav Yisrael*.

Through it all, Yitzchak continued to blossom; he even began his "career" as a *marbitz Torah* at the age of 13, when he delivered a Chumash and Rashi *shiur* at night to the younger boys.

During one ordeal after another, Yitzchak turned to his *siddur*, where he found solace and comfort, for he knew that Hashem was with him, always and everywhere.

Still, under the watchful eye of the institution, he was prevented from going to a real yeshivah. And he wanted nothing more. One day, he and a friend made the bold decision to run away. At the train station, however, they were stopped by the administrator, who had been tipped off about their plans and brought them back to the school.

The following morning, they ran away again.

Yitzchak was now free. But because he was only able to grab a few things, in his haste, he forgot some very important items.

Including his precious *siddur*.

The gift his father had given him on that fateful day was gone.

At first, Yitzchak was crestfallen. But then he realized, there was no need to be.

The message his father had lovingly inscribed was already embedded in his heart.

He had been through so much. And his journey was not yet over. But he knew he was in good hands.

"Daven to Hashem and you will find Him — always and everywhere."

That message would stay with him.

Always and everywhere.

A Secret in Sanz

WHEN RAV SHMUEL DREICHTER WAS A YOUNG MAN, he had a strong desire to travel from Germany to Sanz to see the Divrei Chaim, Rav Chaim Halberstam. Although he did not come from a Chassidic background and Sanz was a metropolis of Chassidus, Shmuel knew that the Rebbe *hut ge'poelt* (had effected) multiple *yeshuos* and he wanted a *berachah* from such an individual.

He asked his father permission to travel, not knowing how he would reply. To Shmuel's joy, his father granted permission and even agreed to fund the trip, on one condition: Shmuel could remain in Sanz for only one day. Upon receiving his father's permission, Shmuel was elated; he would get to meet the famous *tzaddik,* whose wisdom and brilliance were matched only by his kindness and warmth.

In order to fulfill his father's stipulation, Shmuel did some research on how to maximize his time in Sanz and minimize his travel time. The big day arrived and after a half-day of travel, he finally reached Sanz. He asked around for someone to guide him to the home of the Divrei Chaim and he was pointed in the proper direction.

When he arrived, he approached the *gabbai* and asked for an appointment, explaining that he had only one day in town. Much to his chagrin, he was told he would have to wait one week in order to see the Divrei Chaim. Shmuel was so disappointed, but what was there to do? Hundreds of others had also traveled to receive a *berachah* from the Sanzer, as he was known. There were only so many hours in the day and the Rebbe, of course, also needed time for his own *avodas Hashem*. There was no way around it. He was not going to get in any earlier.

Shmuel began to think of an alternate plan. He knew he couldn't delay his return; he had given his father his word. But even if he couldn't obtain a private appointment, there had to be another way. Then he realized that nothing was stopping him from standing outside the Rebbe's door, as close as he possibly could, before it was time to go home.

The *gabbaim* did not protest and allowed Shmuel to stand just outside the door — but he could not open it. As he stood there, he listened carefully and heard the Divrei Chaim reciting a *tefillah* with tremendous *kavanah* and *hislahavus,* concentration and passion. He leaned a little closer so he could make out the words: "*Asher... yatzar... es... ha'adam...*" Each word was enunciated and articulated, accompanied by cries of yearning and *dveikus.*

Shmuel stood transfixed. He had never heard anything like this in his entire life. It sounded like Rav Chaim was davening *Ne'ilah,* only with more concentration, if that was possible. Finally, after 20 minutes, Rav Chaim finished his *berachah.*

Suddenly, the door opened. There he was.

The Divrei Chaim.

Shmuel's knees shook. He had heard so much about the legendary Rebbe, and here he was, right in front of him! The Rebbe called out, "*Shalom aleichem,* Reb Yid from *Deutschland* (Germany)! I want you to know that it was worthwhile for you to come from Germany just to hear how a Yid should make an *Asher Yatzar.*"

Shmuel could hardly believe it. He'd thought he would be unable to see Rav Chaim and now, with almost no intervention, the Rebbe was speaking directly to him.

The Rebbe continued, "Listen to me, *ti'ere bachur'l.* A Yid must have more *kavanah* when he recites the *berachah* of *Asher Yatzar* than when he davens *U'Nesaneh Tokef* on Rosh Hashanah and Yom Kippur! Do you know why?

"Because *U'Nesaneh Tokef* is a *minhag be'alma,* just a custom, and *Asher Yatzar* is a *takanah* of *Chazal.* Not only that, but one can generate more *yeshuos* and *refuos* through *Asher Yatzar* than through *U'Nesaneh Tokef*!"

With that, the Sanzer turned around and went back into his inner chamber.

Here was someone who very possibly knew more about *yeshuos* and *refuos* than almost anyone else alive — and he'd shared his secret. Instead of the reverent prayer in which we speak about life and death at the most exalted moments of the year, Rav

Chaim had instructed Shmuel to concentrate on the *tefillah* recited after the most mundane moments of the day.

> *This message resonated for the rest of Rav Shmuel's life. When he grew older and became a tzaddik in his own right, he continued to share the secret he had heard from the Rebbe of Sanz.*

***

Rav Elya Lopian, the famed mashgiach and *mussar* personality, once traveled with his *talmid* by train from Yerushalayim to Haifa. At the beginning of the trip, the *talmid* asked Rav Elya if one is obligated to recite *tefillas haderech* on this train ride. Rav Elya responded in the affirmative.

A short while later, Rav Elya stood up to go to the washroom. When he came out, he washed his hands and motioned to one of the policemen to gather all the other police officers. When they were all in front of him, he said, "Now I am going to recite *Asher Yatzar.* Please make sure to say Amen."

Though none of them were observant, they all listened carefully as Rav Elya enunciated every word of the *berachah* and then they responded with a resounding Amen. One of them remarked wryly, "After hearing such a *berachah,* one can become a full-fledged *baal teshuvah.*"

A few minutes passed. The train abruptly came to a stop. No one was sure what happened. But slowly, word began to spread. A bomb had been planted under one of the train tracks, and the conductor had somehow noticed it and managed to stop the train at the last moment. Had the train continued for even a few meters, the bomb would have exploded, and there's no telling how many people would have been killed!

The others on the train looked toward Rav Elya, whom they credited for the miracle, to see his reaction, but he had not even looked up from his Gemara during the entire commotion. Only a while later, he noticed the train had stopped and asked his *talmid* what happened. After being informed of the miraculous events, Rav Elya humbly replied, "Now you see how important it was to say *tefillas haderech.*"

U'mafli laasos indeed.

How Far Can It Take You

WHILE DRIVING DOWN I-95 NORTH, I PULLED INTO the Joyce Kilmer Rest Area and ran into the minimart to buy a Diet Dr. Pepper. The man standing in front of me, who appeared to be in his early 60s, was a real character. His shirt was just a tad too tight; his jokes were not nearly as funny as he thought they were; and with a big, bushy mustache, sunglasses covering his eyes, keys dangling out of his pants belt loop, and his baseball hat pulled down right around his eyes, you couldn't have painted a better picture of a trucker.

He seemed to have all the time in the world. It wasn't his fault I was in a rush, so I laughed politely at his jokes as he kept talking to me about nothing. Though the line was growing smaller, I began thinking about dropping my need for a soda and running out the door. The conversation was taking its toll and I really needed to get on my way.

Out of the blue, he turned to me and asked, "Are you a rabbi?"

I wasn't sure what to answer, though it was fairly obvious.

Yarmulke? Check.

Tzitzis out? Check.

Beard? Check.

White shirt, black pants? Check.

I knew he wasn't going to ask me where or when I received *semichah,* so I made things simpler and answered in the affirmative.

"Do you want to hear a good story?"

Now I was getting suspicious. Did he know I collect stories? Was someone videoing this to see how I would react?

Again, I answered yes. As if I had a choice.

So the man introduced himself. "My name is David and I don't know if you could tell, but I drive a truck, though I am also a carpenter," and then he proceeded to tell his story. "A few years ago, I was driving up near Connecticut and was completely lost. I tried to figure out where I was by pulling into a driveway and Googling my location. Suddenly, a man who was obviously a rabbi, along with his wife, walked toward my truck and asked me what I was doing in his driveway. I told him I was trying to discover my location.

"But he waved off that response. 'No, I am asking you: What are you doing here?'

"I tried again. 'My name is David, I'm a truck driver and carpenter, and I'm completely lost.' Then I threw him a joke and asked him and his wife, 'Why? Did you just ask G-d for a carpenter?'"

David was loving his joke and let out a boisterous laugh as he told the story. I could just picture the scene. Then he continued the story.

"But the rabbi didn't laugh at all. He confirmed that indeed he and his wife had just asked G-d for a carpenter. They told me they had several things that needed to be fixed around the house, and as they often did when they needed something done, they turned to G-d and asked Him to send them a carpenter. And as so often happened, one pulled up to the driveway soon after they made the request. Naturally, I agreed to do whatever work they needed. Over the next three weeks, I took care of various jobs in their home. But

I was really impressed with the rabbi and his method of turning to G-d for his needs."

Now that David had finished his story, he turned his attention to me. "Let me ask you a question. Why do you think I'm always meeting rabbis? It's not only you and the rabbi in Connecticut. Though I don't hang out in Jewish communities or in Jewish circles, I often come across rabbis. So what do you think it is?"

Even though his last name was anything but a Jewish name, I instinctively asked him, "Are you by any chance Jewish?"

"Not really."

I said to him, "It doesn't work that way. Either you're Jewish or you're not Jewish."

David then let me know that even though his dad is not Jewish, his mom is. "Even so, I'm not really Jewish because we never did anything Jewish while I was growing up."

"If your mother is Jewish," I explained, "you are a full-fledged Jew. Perhaps that's the reason you keep on meeting rabbis. You don't have to necessarily do anything Jewish to be Jewish."

David had his own possible interpretation of the events, an interpretation I found fascinating. "You know, a while ago I asked my mother why I keep bumping into rabbis. She had her own reason. 'Only once in my life did I go inside a synagogue to pray, and that was when I was expecting you some 60 years ago. I was having difficulty during my pregnancy, and the doctor told me that things weren't looking good; there was a chance my child wouldn't make it. He told me a healthy outcome would take a lot of prayer. I had never prayed before, but I decided this was as good a time as any to turn to G-d. So I went into the synagogue and poured out my heart. You were born healthy and I never went back. But still,' my mom concluded, 'you never know how far one prayer can take you...'"

David had me. I was extremely moved by what I had just heard.

By now, it was his turn at the cashier. He turned to me one last time. "Rabbi, what do you say? You think that may be it?"

I told him there's a good chance. However, after a quick picture, he had to go. As I walked to my car, I called out once more but it was noisy in the parking lot and he couldn't hear me.

I just wanted to tell him, "Keep searching, David. You just may find what you're looking for!"

Striking a Deal

RAV FAIVEL KATZ, ROSH KOLLEL OF KOLLEL YAD CHAIM Mordechai in Beachwood, Ohio, has a son named Ari. Ari, who has special needs, goes to public school during the week and joins a yeshivah on Sundays, when his school is closed. The ultimate goal is to mainstream Ari into a Jewish day school.

The Katzes spend their summers in Camp Agudah Midwest in South Haven, Michigan, where Rav Faivel is involved in the mesivta program. Each summer, Ari soaks up the wonderful, frum atmosphere, delighted to spend so much time with other Jewish children his age.

A few years ago, Rav Faivel asked one of the boys in the camp's mesivta program, Gershon, to learn with Ari. Aside from the benefit for Ari, Rav Faivel knew that Gershon, who was not the strongest student and could use a confidence boost, would gain from learning with Ari and helping him grow.

Every day during learning groups, Gershon and Ari learned together. The *chavrusashaft* was a smashing success — for both parties involved. Even though Ari benefited more, Gershon, too, felt fulfilled. Rav Faivel and his wife were extremely grateful and wanted to express their *hakaras hatov*. However, at the end of the summer, Gershon wouldn't take any money for all the time and effort he had invested in learning with Ari.

The following summer, Rav Faivel arranged once more for Ari to learn with Gershon and although the *chavrusashaft* again worked out beautifully, Gershon still refused to take any money. Rav Faivel couldn't understand why Gershon was so adamant. Nonetheless, he appreciated his kindness.

Right before the summer of 2021, Rav Faivel reached out to Gershon and asked him to learn with Ari for the third summer in a row. Once again, he readily agreed, with the stipulation: Absolutely no money. Not one penny.

"For years now," he explained, "much to my embarrassment and consternation, I had trouble finding *chavrusos.* Sometimes, I would land a really good *chavrusa,* only to get ditched soon after. Most often, though, it didn't even get to that point. After this happened again and again, I finally sat down and made a deal with Hashem: '*Ribbono Shel Olam*, I will serve as a good *chavrusa* for one of Your special children, and I ask that You find a good *chavrusa* for me in return.'

"You should know," Gershon said to Rav Faivel, "that for the past two years, ever since I began learning with Ari, I landed the best *chavrusos,* and my learning has been remarkable."

Then he updated Rav Faivel on his most recent *chavrusa* experience in Yeshivas Mir in Yerushalayim. "At the beginning of Elul, as in most yeshivos, the Mir has a *chavrusa* tumult, where everyone chooses his *chavrusa* for the *zman*. As you can imagine, all of my feelings of inadequacy and fear of rejection came to the fore, causing me intense anxiety. Would I be *zocheh* to a good year of learning, to a good *chavrusa*?"

Gershon seemed to be reliving the story, along with all the stress and strain. "While I had some leads, as the *chavrusa* tumult died down so did my opportunities; four boys, at different points in the day, had told me no. There I was, the day before the *zman*, *chavrusa*-less! So I sat down in the *beis midrash* and spoke to

Hashem, tears coursing down my cheeks. '*Ribbono Shel Olam*! We made a deal! I kept my end of the bargain and learned with Ari, but where is Your end of the deal? I don't have a *chavrusa*!'

"I'm telling you, Rav Faivel, less than 30 seconds later, a *shoel u'meishiv* from the yeshivah came over to me and said, 'Don't ask! I thought I had a *chavrusa,* but the guy just told me we're not learning. You look like someone who needs a *chavrusa*. Would you learn with me?'"

Gershon finished his story as Rav Faivel drank it all in. "Not only did I have a terrific *zman* with that *chavrusa*, but learning with a *chashuve shoel u'meishiv* established me as a sought-after learning partner.

"So Rav Faivel, of course I'll learn with Ari. And I'm *never* taking money!"

Oy! Shema Yisrael!

SHORTLY AFTER THE MARRIAGE OF RAV GOEL ELKARIFF, Rav Shach, rosh yeshivah of Yeshivas Ponovezh, proposed that Rav Goel and fourteen other *yungerleit* from Ponovezh move to Givat Shmuel, a secular neighborhood near Bnei Brak, and start a kollel there.

The proposal seemed so far-fetched. A kollel in Givat Shmuel? This was not something that the community requested, so what could they accomplish? Whom would they be able to influence? How could Torah blossom in the desert?

Nevertheless, the rosh yeshivah felt strongly that this could work, and when Rav Shach sent you somewhere, there was not much room for discussion. Armed with Rav Shach's vote of confidence and blessings for success, and hoping for a large dose of *siyata d'Shmaya,* Rav Goel and the rest of the group moved out to Givat Shmuel. The majority took modest apartments in one building and a few others in an adjacent one.

This was not meant as an outreach kollel. Rav Shach instructed them to learn with each other, hoping that the *kedushah* would permeate the community and enhance the *ruchniyus* of the neighborhood. Although there was an adjustment period for the young couples, soon enough they felt they were making inroads. Rav Goel and his group were polite and non-judgmental and possessed a youthful, contagious exuberance. The backlash and negativity they were initially concerned about never developed.

One of Rav Goel's neighbors, an old Russian Yid, passed him in the hallway every day. Though Rav Goel was friendly, he still didn't feel like he had developed enough of a rapport to strike up a conversation with the man.

But one day, the elderly fellow volunteered, "You know, I'm a *maamin*. I believe in Hashem." Since he had initially assumed otherwise, Rav Goel was happy to hear that his assumption had been incorrect. Yet he wasn't sure how to respond to such a blunt statement, so he nodded his head and waited for the Yid to continue.

"In fact, when I hear you sing Shabbos *zemiros*, it warms my heart. And I am so jealous when you go to the *beit knesset*. I wish I knew how to daven enough to join you." Now Rav Goel was very surprised. He began to feel guilty that he had not invited the man to his home for a Shabbos meal. Apparently, his neighbor would have very much appreciated the invitation, and Rav Goel and his wife had more than enough food.

Before Rav Goel could continue on his guilt trip, however, the Russian Yid began to share his story.

> *During World War II, when I was a young man, I served in the Russian Army. While the Germans boasted sophisticated weaponry, we suffered from a shortage of munitions. Yet*

Stalin, with little value for human life, kept sending thousands of soldiers to the frontlines, as the Germans gunned them down. In addition, it was fairly common for us to chance upon a minefield, and we had no machinery with which to detect mines. Many soldiers were blown up walking across the fields. Between the casualties from the Nazis' firearms and the fatalities from the minefields, every day there were more and more soldiers who would never see their loved ones again.

I, too, was instructed to cross minefields, bullets whizzing by my head. As I took my first step, I searched my memory for something, anything, to hold onto, to give me some strength and hope, and I remembered something my mother used to say when I was a child. She wasn't speaking directly to me. To tell you the truth, I'm not sure to whom she was speaking. But whenever she had some sort of problem or someone was in danger, she would cry out, "Oy! Shema Yisrael! Oy! Shema Yisrael!"

I'm embarrassed to tell you that I didn't even know the end of the pasuk, yet I'd heard those two words over and over and over again as a child. Now that my own life was hanging in the balance, I followed my mother's lead and cried out from the depths, "Oy! Shema Yisrael! Oy! Shema Yisrael!"

As I walked, I braced for the worst. Every tentative step could be my last. Yet somehow — miraculously, of course — every step I took brought me closer to the other end of the field, away from the mines and away from the bullets. And then, I made it. Day after day. Though thousands of soldiers fell from the mines and the bullets all around me, it was as if I were walking between the pitfalls, for no bullet and no mine ever harmed me.

"I knew there could be only one reason that I lived," concluded Rav Goel's neighbor. "It was because of '*Oy! Shema Yisrael!*' I sensed that there is a Creator watching over me, even though I couldn't even recite a full *pasuk*."

Upon hearing this spellbinding account, Rav Goel was reminded of a thought from Rav Chatzkel Abramsky. We say every day in davening, "Shomer Yisrael, shemor she'eiris Yisrael, ve'al yovad Yisrael ha'omrim Shema Yisrael — Guardian of Yisrael, protect the remnant of Yisrael; do not let Yisrael be destroyed, those who proclaim, Shema Yisrael."

These words can also be understood homiletically: Hashem watches over the faithful Jews in Klal Yisrael, even those who are on the she'eiris, on the outskirts, who don't keep the Torah on a daily basis. And even those who are so far removed that the only thing they know is how to say just two words, Shema Yisrael... Hashem looks after them, too.

May Hashem continue to watch over all of us!

Of Socks and Sandwiches

Filled with many chachamim, tzaddikim, and mekubalim, the city of Aleppo, or Aram Tzova, was a bastion of spirituality for Syrian Jews for centuries. However, in the 20th century, the majority of them made their way to Eretz Yisrael and reestablished themselves in Tzefat and Yerushalayim. Their presence enhanced the Sephardic communities of the Holy Land, and the communities prospered and grew.

ON THE FOURTH OF NISSAN, 1934, TRAGEDY STRUCK IN the Syrian community of Yerushalayim. Rav Ezra Abadi-Zahav, a young chacham, passed away at the age of 27, dealing a crushing blow to his wife, Massouda, the daughter of Rav Yehuda Pessya, and their only daughter, Esther. A few months later, the young widow gave birth to another daughter whom she named Victoria. Massouda and her daughters lacked the basics and suffered from hunger and malnutrition. Soon, tragedy struck again when Esther, the older daughter, starved to death.

When little Victoria was only 3 1/2 years old, she asked her mother in all innocence, "Ima, why do all my friends come to school with a sandwich and a fruit, while I bring only a fruit or a vegetable, but sometimes nothing at all? Why can't I also have a sandwich?"

Massouda felt very dejected by the question. She couldn't hold back her tears and had a hard time grabbing ahold of herself. After a few moments, she finally regained her composure and answered her young daughter with the truth. "Victoria dear, all of your friends have a father. When they want something, they ask him for it and he does his best to take care of them. You, my dear daughter, also had a father who was a big *tzaddik,* but he passed away before you were born. So where can we turn?"

Massouda stroked her little girl's face, who should have been too young for this conversation. But since Victoria was wise beyond her years, her mother continued her explanation. "So listen to me, my dear daughter. You do have a father even now, a Father in Heaven, who looks out for his little daughter, the *yetomah*. You know what? You can ask Him for anything you want. He is the Father of all *yetomim* and he has the ability to give you whatever you ask for. Even a sandwich and even an apple."

The little girl took every word her mother said seriously. Walking outside, she lifted her eyes toward Heaven and cried out with a broken heart, "Abba! Abba in Heaven! All the girls in my kindergarten have a father, and I don't have one. My mother told me that You are my Father, and You are the strongest and biggest Father in the world. I know You love me very much, so please listen to me. I'm begging You to please give my mother enough money to support us, so she can buy me a sandwich and an apple for school. Please, Father! Please!"

Finished with her prayer, Victoria skipped away to play. A few minutes later, she went back to her house and told her mother, "Ima, I just want you to know that I spoke to our Father. Just as you told me, I asked Him if He could help support us. I know He's going to listen to me. Tomorrow, you'll send me to school with a sandwich and an apple." Massouda couldn't get over her daughter's sincerity and purity. Dovetailing on Victoria's earnest prayer, Massouda put in her own request for *parnassah*.

No prayer goes unanswered. A half-hour later, there was a knock on her door. It wasn't a pleasant knock, more like a pounding. Massouda quickly went to the door and peeked through the hole. A whole group of Turkish soldiers was standing on the other side. Trembling, she opened it.

"Ma'am," a gruff and muscular officer began without preamble, "the word on the street is that you are a seamstress, and an expert one at that. The men in my unit could use your help. Their heavy woolen socks are torn and as they face the harsh winter months, they cannot go about with holes in their socks. We need you to fix them immediately. We are willing to pay for your work, and we will pay for it ahead of time."

The officer placed two gold coins on the table, along with a sack of torn woolen socks. He told Massouda he'd be back in a few days to collect them all. Though she was excited about the work, and overjoyed that she had received well over the going rate, Massouda wondered if she could get the job in time. With no other option, she began to work and kept going, until she finished darning every last sock. Then she waited for the soldiers to return.

They never would.

A few days after the soldiers brought the socks, General Allenby and his men entered Jerusalem. The Turkish Army fled and never returned. The two gold coins were enough to support Massouda and her daughter for a long, long time.

Victoria's innocent plea worked instantly.

And the following day, yes, Victoria brought a sandwich of her own to school.

Along with an apple.

Victoria and her mother knew they always had Someone to turn to.

Victoria married the tzaddik, Rav Yosef Batzri, and they were zocheh to exceptional children, Rav Menachem, Rav Sasson, and Rav Dovid, who have illuminated the Sephardic Torah world.

Pipe Cleaners

There is one thing we all pray for, one thing everybody wants: a beautiful home. No, I'm not talking about a beautifully furnished home. I'm talking about a beautiful family, with beautiful children.

It's everyone's dream.

WHEN RAV YEHUDA SCHWAB, THE FATHER OF THE exceptional Schwab children — Rav Shimon, Rav Mordechai, Rav Moshe, Rav Chaim Tzvi, and Rav Yitzchak — was asked, "How were you *zocheh* to such a beautiful family?" at first he replied, "I don't know."

However, after a bit of thought, he said, "There's one thing I do know. Before my *chuppah*, I asked the *Ribbono Shel Olam* to make a deal with me. I promised that I would bring *kavod,* honor and beauty, to His home by not talking in shul, and asked Him to reciprocate by bringing *kavod,* honor and beauty, to mine."

Rav Yehuda kept his end of the bargain, and the *Ribbono Shel Olam* kept His. The Schwab family has always been *le'sheim u'l'siferes,* a magnificent *mishpachah.*

Not talking in shul can serve as the source of berachah in many ways.

Rav Meir Michoel Greenwald, a *chashuve Yid* in Eretz Yisrael, has taken it upon himself to spread awareness of *kedushas beis haknesses.* He and his brother were once traveling together in a car, when his brother got a call. In truth, the person on the other line, Reb Menachem, was a good friend of Rav Greenwald and would usually call him on his own cell phone, but for some reason, this time he didn't. Rav Greenwald's brother answered the phone and Reb Menachem asked to speak to Rav Greenwald. When Rav Greenwald asked Reb Menachem why he called his brother's phone and not his own, Reb Menachem himself didn't know why.

But there was a reason.

Reb Menachem explained to Rav Greenwald that he was sitting next to a man named Reb Yehoshua, whose father was suffering from liver disease. Reb Yehoshua had heard that Rav Greenwald has a repertoire of stories about individuals who were healed from liver ailments when they or those close to them committed not to talk in shul, and he was eager for some *chizuk*. But first, Reb Menachem, the middleman, had a question. "Tell me, what is the connection between liver disease and a shul?"

Rav Greenwald replied, "I'll explain the connection, but afterward I would like to speak directly to Reb Yehoshua, the ill man's son. So this is the explanation: Someone who gives כבוד, honor, to the *Shechinah* does not speak in the *beis haknesses* at the time of *tefillah.* כבד , the liver, corresponds to כבוד, and the liver is thereby cured."

Simple enough.

Now it was time to pass the phone to Reb Yehoshua, who repeated his request to hear stories. "I'll be happy to tell you many stories," Rav Meir Michoel responded. "But please tell me. Where does your father daven?"

After Reb Yehoshua told him the name of the place, Rav Meir Michoel stated, "I have a secret to tell you."

Curious, Reb Yehoshua asked, "Secret? What kind of secret?"

"In the shul where your father davens, all the pipes are clogged."

"Clogged pipes?" He had no idea what he was referring to. "Are you a plumber? I'm not looking for plumbing assistance. I don't care about the pipes. I just want my father to have a *refuah sheleimah*."

"Actually, I am a plumber," countered Rav Meir Michoel.

"And how's that?"

Rav Greenwald sensed that Reb Yehoshua was eager to hear what he had to say. "Chazal tell us that when we pray, it is an עת רצון, an opportune time, to come close to Hashem and make requests of Him. The word רצון has the same letters as the word for pipe, צנור. But if people talk during davening, all the pipes become clogged and we lose out on our *eis ratzon*. I've been trying to help people unclog their pipes, to mitigate the damage. Each person who talks harms not only himself, but others, as well."

Reb Yehoshua was a tad insulted. "You're saying that my father is one who causes harm to others?"

Rav Greenwald clarified.

The Gemara (Bava Kama 3b) discusses four primary sources of damage, one of which is מבעה*, an acronym for:* מדבר בזמן עת התפילה*, one who speaks at the time of prayer; such a person causes tremendous damage.*

In the Gemara, Rav states what מבעה *is referring to and explains his reasoning: The word* מבעה *is rooted in the words from Yeshayah (21:12),"* אם תבעיון בעיו *— If you really desire it, ask for it," alluding to the requests we make during tefillah.*

Furthermore, according to the Maharsha, the nation of Edom represents the koach hacherev, the power of the sword. And how are we saved from the sword of Edom, of Eisav? אם תבעיון*, through tefillah. As Yitzchak said (Bereishis 27:22),*

"Hakol kol Yaakov ve'hayadayim yedei Eisav — The voice is Yaakov's voice but the hands are Eisav's hands"; when the voice of Yaakov is powerful, the hands of Eisav have no dominion over him.

Rav Greenwald concluded, "If we speak during *tefillah,* Eisav gains the upper hand, which brings about all kinds of ruin, destruction, and suffering."

Just then, Rav Greenwald's phone rang. Rav Greenwald, who was speaking on his brother's phone, asked Reb Yehoshua to wait a moment as he took the call from overseas.

The caller asked, "Are you the Rav Greenwald who speaks about the prohibition of speaking during davening?"

As Rav Greenwald replied in the affirmative, the caller began sharing an astonishing story. All of a sudden, Reb Yehoshua called out from Rav Greenwald's brother's phone: "What's going on?" wondering why he was being pushed aside for so long.

To resolve the issue, Rav Greenwald put both phones on speaker mode, and Reb Yehoshua also listened to the extraordinary story of the man from overseas:

Seven years ago, you gave a shmuess about the kavod we owe to our shuls, and how we must refrain from speaking during davening. I attended the lecture and I haven't spoken in shul since. Two years ago, a close family member was diagnosed with liver cancer, with a grim prognosis. At that time, I accepted upon myself not to speak divrei chol in shul at all, even when it wasn't during davening.

Two weeks later, the cancer cells spread to half of my relative's liver; his condition was critical. There was no choice but to cut out half of the liver, and to do it immediately. If not, his chances of survival were nil. With no other options, the family gave their consent.

A couple of weeks after the operation, the tests revealed that the remaining portion of the liver was completely cancer-free. A person can live with half of a liver, as it regenerates on its own. To the joy of his fellow congregants, my relative returned to shul, completely back to himself.

Recognizing the miracle, many young men in the shul committed to stop speaking during davening. They had witnessed the capacity of this kabbalah and now wanted to be a part of this revolution!

Recently, at the end of the summer, my relative began feeling unwell. He took some tests and received devastating results: The cancer had returned. The situation deteriorated until I got a call right before Rosh Hashanah that he was near death; it was time to go to the hospital to say a final goodbye.

Instead, I decided to go to the shul in which so many people had taken upon themselves not to talk during davening. I opened the aron kodesh and cried, "Ribbono Shel Olam, in this place, tens of Jews stopped talking during davening. If my relative dies, what will I tell all these people? I, too, promised not to speak divrei chol in this shul, and I haven't uttered a word since I made the commitment. Ribbono Shel Olam, I am not davening only for the sake of the choleh, but to ask that no chillul Hashem should come of this!" I closed the aron and went home to prepare for Rosh Hashanah.

Not more than 10 minutes later, I received a call from the doctor. My relative had shown slight improvement. On the first day of Rosh Hashanah, he opened his eyes, and on the second day, he asked for a glass of water. A short while later, fully recovered, he was discharged from the hospital!

Hearing this, Rav Greenwald directed his words to Reb Yehoshua: "Quickly, bring a plumber to your father's shul and fix the clogged pipes! Have the entire shul accept upon themselves not to speak in middle of davening!"

He did.

Soon, the pipes were clear.

And his father was cured.

CHESED

If the Shoe Fits!

RAV BINYAMIN DINOVITZ SERVED AS RAV OF OHEL Yakov Congregation in Baltimore for over 50 years. In the 1960s, Rav Dinovitz worked hard to raise his family. Financially, it was not easy, certainly not for a rav.

Despite his young age, Rav Dinovitz began to experience foot problems. After seeing several doctors, he was advised to buy special therapeutic socks to help alleviate the pain. However, his tight budget did not allow for extras. When weighed against necessities like food, rent, and tuition, therapeutic socks fell into the luxury category. In order to afford the precious socks, he put aside money, a bit every week, until he had enough to buy five pairs of therapeutic socks.

Rav Binyamin's reputation as a sensitive and caring individual made his home a common stop for those seeking assistance. Although he was not able to give large sums of money, he was able to give a listening ear, a shoulder to cry on, and an enormous heart.

One day, a needy fellow came to Rav Binyamin's door, seeking advice on an important matter. During the course of the conversation, the man shared that he had recently begun suffering from foot ailments. Soon enough, Rav Binyamin realized that he and the man suffered from the same type of pain. Not only that, but the man had also been advised to buy special socks.

Yes, the same socks Rav Binyamin had recently purchased.

Immediately, Rav Binyamin called in his son Peretz and instructed him to retrieve the bag of socks he had just acquired. Peretz was old enough to know that his father had saved money to buy the socks and that they were very necessary for his comfort and well-being. But he also knew how generous his father was. So he quickly made his way to the bag of socks and took out two pairs of socks — for his father — leaving only three to give to their guest.

He brought the bag to his father, who looked inside. Noticing that two pairs were missing, he again sent Peretz to his room and asked him to find the two missing pairs. Recognizing what he was up against, Peretz returned a moment later with the last two pairs. His father put them in the bag and happily handed them to his visitor.

If need be, Rav Binyamin would suffer. But at least he was able to ease the discomfort and pain of a fellow Jew.

***

Rav Dinovitz's foot issues extended to his arches. At a certain point, the pain became so acute that it was difficult to go about his daily routine. Then someone suggested a local woman, a widow, who sold custom-made orthopedic shoes and took pride in her work. Rav Dinovitz called and asked her to fashion a pair for him. Although it was going to be expensive, it would be worth it — for him physically and for her financially. A win-win situation, in his view. After saving up for this purchase, Rav Dinovitz took the money and, along with his son Peretz, went to be fitted.

The woman prepared a mold for his feet and promised Rav Binyamin that the shoes would be ready in three weeks. She assured him they would be worth the money and the wait, as they would reduce his pain and enhance his functionality. Rav Binyamin paid in full and waited anxiously for the final product.

Finally, the day arrived, and he and his son drove to the woman's home. Though she suggested he try on the shoes first to make sure they fit properly, Rav Dinovitz didn't want to go through the painstaking process of taking off his shoes and putting on the new ones, so he thanked the woman and took the shoes without trying them on.

Father and son excitedly looked forward to Rav Dinovitz's relief from his constant pain, but their excitement was short-lived. Try as he might, he was unable to put the shoes on. Rav Dinovitz and Peretz soon came to the unfortunate realization that the shoes had been crafted incorrectly. Rav Dinovitz merely shrugged his shoulders in resignation, but his son suggested the obvious. "Tomorrow, we'll go back to the woman and ask her to make a new pair for you or else refund your money."

A kind and gentle soul, Rav Dinovitz always spoke softly. Not this time. He responded to his son emphatically and strongly. "Absolutely not! *Nebach*, this woman devoted three weeks to making the shoes and this is her only source of income. I can't allow her to lose out. Until now, I've been able to manage, and with continued help from Hashem, I will be all right. But under no circumstances will we bring the shoes back."

He was as good as his word.

Rav Dinovitz passed away in 2008. But those brand-new shoes still sit in his children's home.

A priceless family heirloom.

The Lawbreaker

A young yasom, who had experienced the horrors of the war, traveled to America by ship. As soon as he arrived at Ellis Island, disoriented and unable to speak a word of English, a young man walked right up to him, spoke to him in Yiddish, and asked if he could be of assistance; a familiar tongue gave the orphan some hope and encouragement, and he answered, "I have nothing. No money, no family. Nothing whatsoever."

"From now on, we will take care of everything for you," replied his savior. "We will be your family. Come with me." The boy didn't even know whom he was following, but the invitation was more than welcome.

That young man who invited the lost soul was Rav Naftulchik, whose father, Rav Shlomo Halberstam, was the Bobover Rebbe. Rav Naftulchik brought the orphan boy to his father, who took him under his wing. Ultimately, he would walk him down to the chuppah and help him build a family of his own.

This is what the Rebbe, himself a Holocaust survivor, did for one Yid after another. Those scattered souls would become thousands of vibrant, eager, and devout families. But for now, they were starving, shattered, and homeless. They needed food and clothing. They needed an infusion of life. And the Rebbe was there to give it to them. The Rebbe housed many of these downhearted individuals in the basement of his home. He took care of them and nourished their bodies and souls, mending their hearts and helping them build from scratch.

And from these broken human beings blossomed the beautiful Chassidus of Bobov.

It didn't stop there. The Rebbe continued to care for his Chassidim, and all Yidden, for the rest of his life. Anyone who needed help knew where they could find it; the Rebbe was THE address, ready and willing to help.

IT WAS DURING THIS TIME THAT THE REBBE HEARD OF A group of Jews stranded in Eastern Europe. They, too, had nothing. They didn't have food, clothing, or shelter. In fact, when he researched the matter, the Rebbe discovered that some members of the group were so forlorn that they were prepared to give up, to take their own lives! If this world offered nothing, then why continue to fight? The Rebbe knew he had to do something.

He began working feverishly to obtain the necessary paperwork for these people to come to America. But there was a problem. In order to be allowed entry, those stuck in Europe had to come up with signed affidavits, to prove to the United States government that they would not become a burden to the state. And not enough Jews in America had the wherewithal to vouch for them.

Congressman Sol Bloom, a Jewish congressman, was targeted as the one with whom to plead their case. Numerous attempts were made to influence the congressman's thinking, but those efforts made little impact. A stickler for rules, the congressman was unwilling to bend those laws. When approached, he sympathized deeply with the requests but insisted that the law is the law, and it was strictly forbidden to bring in refugees unless they had someone to provide for them.

The Rebbe was determined to do his utmost. After sending various representatives to argue his case, he arranged to have a personal meeting in Washington DC with the congressman; he was given five minutes. The Rebbe arrived a day before the scheduled meeting, to make sure he was on time. But he had no place to sleep.

If such circumstances arose nowadays, the Rebbe would have an entourage of Chassidim traveling with him and people would be vying to have the Rebbe stay with them. However, immediately after the war, he was on a virtual island. With nowhere to go, the Bobover Rebbe slept in a local shul. The next morning after davening, he went straight to meet with Congressman Bloom.

The clock was ticking. The Rebbe knew he had to grab the congressman's attention, that if he were to introduce himself as Shlomo Halberstam, it would have zero effect and the meeting could be over before it started.

He chose a different tack. "I came to tell you that I am a lawbreaker."

Now he had the congressman's attention.

"I come from a place where the law states that you send all Jews to Auschwitz. You send them there to squeeze the last little bit of work out of them, and when they can no longer work, you throw them into the gas chambers. The law dictates that Jews cannot run away and they cannot hide. They are not permitted, G-d forbid, to steal food, even to save their lives. These are the laws. And during the war, I broke all of these laws.

"Now I stand before you with one request. Are you also prepared to join me to break the law? It's true that American law states that you can't allow refugees into the country, but this law is also causing people to die. It's robbing people of their future. It's causing little children to starve to death. It's a cruel law. And we must find a way to get around it!"

The Rebbe began to cry, unable to control himself.

A few moments passed and he pulled himself together. When he looked up again at the congressman, the congressman didn't say a word, but his eyes locked onto the Rebbe's. He stood up, walked to the other side of his desk, and extended his hand. "Rabbi, I will join you! Tell me what to do."

Congressman Sol Bloom advocated for the Eastern European Jews and fought vigorously for the United States government to accept additional refugees. Together, he and the Rebbe saved many Yidden.

When one really wants to achieve, he will allow nothing to stand in his way.

The proof is in the generations of Jews saved by the Rebbe.

The Note Reader

Rav Shlomo Hoffman, a well-known Torah scholar with a deep understanding of the human mind, was one of the leading mental-health professionals in Eretz Yisrael. Both the religious and secular sectors valued his opinion and held him in the highest regard. Sensitive and pulsating with wisdom, Rav Shlomo helped thousands face their struggles and conquer their demons. He understood people, zeroed in on what was troubling them, diagnosed their issues, and healed their souls. Even when he could not solve their problems, he empathized with the individuals who came to him, feeling their anguish and their angst.

The Spinka Rebbe, one of the many gedolim who consulted Rav Shlomo to gain insight and understanding into the complexities of the human condition, recounted an important story, which he heard from Rav Shlomo.

AS A YOUNG *BACHUR*, SHLOMO LEARNED IN YESHIVAS Chevron in Geulah, where he forged a close relationship with the rosh yeshivah, Rav Isaac Sher. At that time, Shlomo slept in the Beis Yisrael neighborhood, in the home of Rav Shloim'ke of Zhvil. Rav Shloim'ke was known for his tremendous heart. Defeated and dispirited Yidden frequently showed up at his door to bare their hearts and beg for help.

It wasn't unusual for Rav Shloim'ke to discuss an issue with the much younger *Litvishe bachur*. What Shlomo lacked in terms of experience, he more than made up for with his intellect and heart. Rav Shloim'ke understood that this young *bachur* possessed the *techunos hanefesh* (inner qualities) to help many Yidden when he would become older.

One night, Shlomo returned from a full day of learning to find Rav Shloim'ke sitting at his table, a pile of *kvitlach* on his desk, perhaps fifty small notes. This was not unusual; what came next was. Rav Shloim'ke instructed Shlomo to pull up a chair at his table and read the *kvitlach*. Shlomo was more than a bit surprised. He had never read *kvitlach* before; he was just a teenager. Still, not one to argue, he sat down at the table while the Rebbe walked out of the room.

Shlomo picked up the first note, from a man whose three older daughters were long past their prime. Streaks of white had begun to creep into his daughters' hair, driving home the fact that they were not growing any younger and causing them anxiety, worry, and depression. The father begged the Rebbe to intercede on their behalf. Shlomo tried to imagine the sadness of these not-so-young ladies, the heaviness and emptiness in their home. His heart sank; he was about to cry. But it was only the first note. There were so many more to go.

He picked up a second note, revealing the story of a fellow who had run into some very serious debt. He had borrowed all he could and had no way of paying up his loans. He felt like he was suffocating; he had no peace of mind. Shlomo felt a horrible pit forming inside of his stomach, as he began to fathom the man's situation: not one moment free of stress, pressure, and tension — day or night.

He had read only two notes, and already he couldn't bear to pick up another. This was awfully difficult, much harder than he had anticipated. But the Rebbe had asked him to read the *kvitlach*, so he reached for a third note.

In this note, the tremulous handwriting told a harrowing story. A young woman who had been in remission from a serious disease had recently been informed that her illness had returned. She worried about her children and their future. Shlomo let out a deep sigh, an audible *krechtz*. He couldn't bear to read the rest of the note from this sick mother.

He looked at the three notes sitting in a small pile, and the many notes he had not even begun to read. That was when Rav Shloim'ke walked back into the room and asked Shlomo if he had read the *kvitlach*.

Shlomo admitted that he had read a few but was unable to look at any others; he was completely overwhelmed after only three of them. "Rebbe, who can bear the pain of these shattered people?"

The Rebbe spoke with urgency. "So only I have to read of their suffering? No one else has to? On the contrary! Every single Jew must read the *kvitlach* of other Yidden. Maybe they will be able to help them, and maybe they won't.

"Still, everyone must try to feel their pain!"

After recounting the story as he had heard it from Rav Shlomo, the Spinka Rebbe highlighted, "It was at that moment that Rav Shlomo began his journey to becoming a rofei nefashos, a healer of Yiddishe souls."

Over the next 60-plus years, many came to Rav Shlomo's door seeking guidance and advice.

He wasn't able to help them all — but he always felt their pain.

Be an Angel

AFTER WRITING DOWN HIS *CHIDDUSHEI TORAH* FOR many years, Reb Yonasan, a young *talmid chacham* from Eretz Yisrael, decided to publish them. As he prepared them for print, he went through his notes over and over again, elucidating his thoughts and proofing for mistakes. Finally, he felt the manuscript was ready for publication.

But before printing, he wanted a *tzaddik*'s *haskamah*. Since Reb Yonasan lived near the Be'er Yaakov of Nadvorna, he made an appointment and showed the Rebbe the *gilyonos*, the pages of *chiddushei Torah*. The Rebbe looked them over and was very impressed, praising Reb Yonasan and commenting on how he must have come from a home of Torah and *hasmadah*.

Reb Yonasan replied that this was not the case. He did not come from a home where Torah was learned. Far from it, in fact.

Then he told his story.

I grew up in a secular home in Ramat Gan. While my father was completely uninvolved and totally removed from Yiddishkeit, my mother was a little more connected but still mostly unobservant. Nevertheless, a small spark of Yiddishkeit flickered inside of her, and occasionally she acted upon it.

One Simchas Torah, she decided to bring me to Kiryas Vizhnitz for hakafos, two kilometers (about a mile and a quarter) from my home. While it was by no means a short walk for a little boy, it was doable.

The night of Simchas Torah arrived and I dressed for the occasion, with a nicer than usual shirt and pair of pants, plus sandals instead of sneakers. As we walked, I held my mother's hand, anticipating something special, though I wasn't really sure what to expect.

As we walked up to the impressive marble edifice, I took note of the hustle and bustle. Hundreds of families were walking around, many pushing strollers, their children holding toy Sifrei Torah, flags, and bags of treats.

My mother knew she couldn't bring me into the beis midrash, so she told me to walk in myself. Drawn toward the singing and dancing, I made my way up the many stairs into the building and then into the beis midrash. As a small boy among many adults, it was hard to see where I was going, yet I followed the crowd into the beis midrash, which was filled with boys around my age and men crowned with shtreimlach. All having a wonderful time. The palpable energy made me want to jump right in.

But how, and with whom? I was just a little boy standing awkwardly, lost and alone. There were bags of candy, flags flying in the air, and children jumping up and down. And then there was me.

No yarmulke. No payos. Empty-handed. No parent there to guide me. I can still remember the overwhelming feelings of loneliness and disorientation.

As I stood there, all the little boys began running toward their fathers, who bent down and lifted them up onto their shoulders. It was the sixth hakafah: hakafas yeladim, the children's hakafah; the Vizhnitzer Chassidim have the minhag of lifting their children onto their shoulders during this hakafah. The excitement reached its height as the children sat there, on top of the world.

But I had nowhere to go. Although my father was alive and well, he had refused to come along. I started to think that perhaps this wasn't such a good idea after all, and maybe I should just turn around and leave.

Out of nowhere, the kindest and warmest man bent down toward me, his eyes radiating love. "Tzaddik'l, do you want to climb up on my shoulders?" My heart skipped a beat; I was so excited that someone noticed me and someone cared. I couldn't believe I was going to be like everyone else. Overcome, all I could do was nod my head. Thankfully, for him it was enough.

He lifted me carefully onto his shoulders and danced with me, asking every minute or two if I was comfortable, if I was all right, did I want to come down. For the next 30 minutes, the man danced with me and jumped with me and sang along with the crowd, "Moshe emes ve'Soraso emes," and I smiled from ear to ear, enjoying every moment. It was an electric atmosphere.

I had never felt so alive and so connected to Yiddishkeit. It had always been portrayed to me, especially by my father, in such a negative light. And now I couldn't get enough of the magic. Even though I didn't know the words, I sang and rejoiced like all the other children, and smiled and laughed. It was one of the most intoxicating moments of my life. I didn't want the hakafah to end; I wished it would last forever, but obviously it didn't. After about a half-hour, it was over, and the tzaddik bent down and eased me off of his shoulders. He smiled at me and I smiled back.

That was the last time I saw him.

"Rebbe," concluded Reb Yonasan, "until today, I don't know the name of that *malach*. But that's the day my life was turned around. Though I was still young, that's the day I decided to become a *ben Torah*."

At times, a Yid may go through hard times, feeling lost and alone. Overwhelmed and disoriented.

If you know someone going through a hard time, you be their malach.

They will never forget it.

And they will never forget you.

Nothing New

Rav Simcha Zelig Riger, the Brisker dayan, was known far and wide as an outstanding posek. In fact, he gave semichah to some of the Torah leaders of the next generation.

During the period in which Rav Simcha Zelig learned in Volozhin, he became close to Rav Chaim Soloveitchik, who held him in high esteem. When Rav Chaim was offered the position of rav in Brisk, he accepted only on condition that Rav Simcha Zelig would become the dayan.

The following story reveals how Rav Simcha Zelig's erudition and brilliance in learning were rivaled by his exceptionally kind, caring, and sensitive behavior toward others.

AS RAV SIMCHA ZELIG AGED, HIS WIFE, WHO WAS OFTEN unwell, was no longer able to live at home. As such, a rotation of *bachurim*, each with a 24-hour shift, was organized to take care of him. They walked him where he needed to go, arranged his meals, and slept in his home at night.

When it was Velvel Eidelman's turn, he presented himself to Rav Simcha Zelig after Shacharis, and then prepared to escort him home. Despite his need for physical assistance, Rav Simcha Zelig still served as the dayan and many people asked him questions. Immediately after Velvel walked over to Rav Simcha Zelig, a young man came over and began to speak to him. But the conversation was not about a kosher chicken or *hilchos Shabbos*. The young man was intent on asking the dayan a string of questions such as: "Am I going to get married? Will it be soon? Will I build a family? Will I have children? Am I going to have money to support my family?"

These types of questions came in rapid-fire succession, and the patient dayan responded to each calmly: Yes, the *bachur* would get married; yes, it would be soon; yes, he would build a family, and so on. In an admirable display of tolerance and understanding, Rav Simcha Zelig did his utmost to reassure the young man, who was obviously struggling with anxiety, that everything would be fine. But what made it even more amazing is that the entire scene repeated itself five minutes later in the same sequence, practically word for word.

Once more, the *bachur* asked questions along the lines of, "Am I going to get married? Will it be soon? Will I build a family? Will I have children? Am I going to have money to support my family?" Plus a few similar questions at the end.

Velvel looked at Rav Simcha Zelig, hoping to receive some guidance as to how to deal with this individual. Should he push him away? Should he ask him to stop bothering Rav Simcha Zelig? Perhaps he should suggest he return in a few hours. But the dayan continued answering the questions as if they were the most normal questions in the world, and as if he were hearing them for the first time. This continued the entire walk back to his home. When the dayan entered his house, the fellow followed. When Rav Simcha Zelig entered the restroom, the agitated young man stood outside. Immediately after the dayan emerged, even before he had a chance to wash his hands, the young man again peppered him with his list of concerns.

Velvel was at his wits' end. He felt responsible to look after Rav Simcha Zelig, and this emotionally challenged young man was beyond annoying. Velvel wondered if he should push the *bachur* out the door. Yes, it's true Rav Simcha Zelig's patience was awe-inspiring, but how much more could he be tested? Thankfully, after a while, the nudnik left the apartment and didn't come back the rest of the day.

Velvel felt it important to inform a family member of what was going on. The next morning, after he escorted Rav Simcha Zelig to davening, Velvel spotted Rav Simcha Zelig's son-in-law and told him of the sequence of events. Much to his surprise, the son-in-law wasn't any more bothered than his father-in-law had been.

Velvel could no longer hide his disbelief. He asked how Rav Simcha Zelig's son-in-law could be so nonchalant about all the nudging Rav Simcha Zelig was subjected to. His son-in-law quickly put the matter to rest. "Do you think this is the first time this happened? He has been doing this every day for the last four months!"

Rav Velvel Eidelman became a giant in his own right, never forgetting the patience he witnessed.

Today, more than ever, people place an emphasis on visiting gedolim, for berachos and for guidance. While it is always special to see how wise and learned they are, we should be no less inspired by the limitless patience they exhibit.

And they do it every day.

Stronger!

The Jewish people are referred to as rachmanim, baishanim, and gomlei chasadim. We are compassionate, shamefaced, and perform acts of kindness (Yevamos 79a). Today, one does not need to look very far in order to carry out acts of kindness. There are hundreds of chesed organizations, providing for every type of need. The opportunities seem endless.

But there were many times in our history — and there still may be times today — when kindness was not easy to come by, when our very basic needs were missing, when we had nothing to share.

Nevertheless, we never forgot that we possess the innate sensitivity to give and provide for others. And if we contemplate how to go about it, we always find a way.

ALTHOUGH THEY HAD HEARD THE RUMORS, THE JEWS of Seret, Romania, had somehow dodged the torment and persecution of the Holocaust when World War II first broke out. That is, until 1941, when the Nazis decided the time had come for Seret to become *Judenrein,* as well. The Romanians, especially as represented by the Iron Guard, were all too willing to assist their

Nazi counterparts in getting rid of their Jewish problem.

To an 11-year-old boy, Berel, the terror and horror came too quickly to process. The Nazis stormed into his town, announcing that the Jews had mere moments to pack their belongings. They were going on a little "hike," the Germans said. The Jewish families frantically packed a few basic belongings and hurried to the town square, where they stood together in the cold, in a driving rainstorm. The Nazi guards, annoyed that they were getting soaked, took out their frustration on their innocent victims, as their ferocious dogs barked violently at the terrified men, women, and children.

Then just like that, they were on their way.

To where? No one knew.

It didn't seem to matter. That wasn't the point of the journey. In truth, the trek, which went on for hours and hours, and then days, seemed pointless. After some time elapsed, the old and weak and sick, desperate for a few drops of water, first cried out and then began to fall, one by one.

Berel knew he had to do something. Of course, he would be risking his life, but doing nothing was not an option. As his feet shuffled beneath him and he tried to keep up with the healthier men and women, he thought long and hard, and then he hit upon an idea.

While no one was looking, he dipped the strings of his *tallis katan* into the frozen swamp nearby. Then he ran over to a weak, elderly individual, who was moaning from thirst and exhaustion, and squeezed the strings until little droplets of water quenched the man's thirst. He repeated his selfless act of kindness for another individual, and then another, and then another. Each time, he soaked the strings and then squeezed out the water into the mouths of his fellow Yidden.

After giving droplets of life to many Yidden, the icy winds caused him to shiver in pain in his wet and frozen *tallis katan*, but nothing could take away Berel's satisfaction. Perhaps the vicious soldiers had the physical strength and ammunition, but this boy had the resilience and sensitivity of a *Yiddishe hartz*, and nothing was stronger.

That sensitive boy survived the war and would never stop feeling for others.

After the war, Berel made his way to Eretz Yisrael, where he became the Nadvorna Rebbe, Rav Yaakov Yissachar Ber Rosenbaum, who helped hundreds of Yidden in his capacity as Rebbe, through his wise counsel, astute advice, and genuine empathy.

Sing It for Me

Yair Yisraeli did not have an easy childhood. When he was just a little baby, his father passed away and a few years later, his mother also died. Raised through the kindness of others, he never forgot the importance of being sensitive to those in need. Rav Yair grew into an exceptional person, a rosh yeshivah of Tiferes Yisrael Yeshivah in Rishon LeZion and a baal chesed extraordinaire.

Rav Yair was beloved by one and all. For many years, he influenced thousands of talmidim, who cherished their rebbi and kept a connection with him long after they left his tutelage. Additionally, many sought out Rav Yair when checking into medical references. He was well connected and informed.

Just to give you an inkling into what type of person Rav Yair was...

On one occasion, he attended a cello recital for a little boy.

It seemed strange that a rosh yeshivah would show up to a musical performance. When someone asked him why he had come, he admitted that he didn't know the family, but he knew the boy was a yasom and the mother an almanah. "Since there was no father to attend, I thought it would be nice if I would go and then compliment the boy on his talent. The mother was so happy I came."

AT THE END OF HIS LIFE, RAV YAIR WAS VERY SICK, CONfined to bed in Mayanei Hayeshua Medical Center. During those days, the *sar haTorah*, Rav Chaim Kanievsky, who felt extremely close to Rav Yair and valued his relationship, visited him.

Yet though his family knew how special Rav Yair was, nothing could prepare them for the greatness they were to witness in the final few days of his life. The doctors informed the family that the situation was dire, and they themselves could see Rav Yair was slowly leaving them. During that time, his family and close *talmidim* stood around his bed. He didn't ask for much; there wasn't much they could do for him.

Although he had been a luminous figure, with an unbridled joy, the illness had taken its toll. Rav Yair had little strength or energy left. When a group of singers made their rounds in the hospital to cheer up the patients, they stopped in Rav Yair's room and asked if he had any requests. At first, he graciously declined.

Then out of the blue, he seemed to change his mind. He cleared his throat and motioned that he had a request — but it was an unusual one.

Rav Yair wanted the choir members to sing a song: a Russian song. Now this was very strange. Either there was something about Rav Yair's childhood his family and *talmidim* were unaware of, or his mind was slipping. However, when he repeated his request, the singers did their best to accommodate him. A few of them knew a Russian folk song and they began singing it to the best of their ability.

Rav Yair smiled; he appeared so happy they were fulfilling his request. When they finished, he asked for another one and they duly cooperated. When they finished that song, he requested one more. With each song the singers sang, the situation seemed more and more bizarre. But soon everyone would understand.

As soon as they finished the third and final song, Rav Yair leaned over. Next to his bed was a curtain. He pulled it away slightly and began conversing with the man in the bed next to him.

A man from Russia.

Although Rav Yair's strength was sapped after the little choir's performance, he smiled at his neighbor and asked if he'd enjoyed the songs.

Had he ever.

Unfortunately, the Russian man had no visitors. While Rav Yair's side of the room was constantly buzzing with activity, his roommate had no one.

In truth, however, he did.

He had Rav Yair.

One day later, Rav Yair returned his *neshamah* to *Shamayim*, after spending his final day on this earth doing his best to bring joy to another Yid.

HASHGACHAH PRATIS

You Can Never Imagine

Wouldn't it be nice to be aware of the Al-mighty's ultimate plan? This way, when misfortunes occur and disappointment plagues us, we can brace ourselves, knowing it will all work out in the end, that there is a reason.

If only it were so easy.

Indeed, the pitfalls and detours of life come our way only for the Al-mighty to get us where we need to be. And if we were truly cognizant of this, and truly believed it at all times, we would have no need to know Hashem's ultimate plan in advance.

The following story, told by Rebbetzin Leah Kolodetsky, is proof of this.

If you were to think of a million possible scenarios, the way this story plays out would never occur to you.

Dear reader, brace yourself. Listen and learn.

A PROMINENT FAMILY IN YERUSHALAYIM WAS BLESSED with seven exceptional boys, one better than the next. They were accepted into one of the most reputable *mosdos* for *yeshivah gedolah*, and they were very successful there. One after another, they made steady advances in yeshivah, developed into outstanding *bnei Torah*, and married wonderful girls from exceptional families.

This went on for the first six boys, up to Eliezer.

When Eliezer, the youngest, went to take his *bechinah* in this same yeshivah, things did not go so smoothly. Though no less outstanding than his older brothers, he was reticent and shy. And on the *bechinah,* he stumbled just a touch.

Even so, he was pretty sure he'd be admitted to the yeshivah and he waited for the acceptance letter, just for confirmation. A few weeks later, he received his answer.

It was a no.

With tears in his eyes, Eliezer stared blankly at the letter. He just couldn't understand why. His parents, who were also baffled, called everyone they knew with connections to the yeshivah, and these people spoke to the members of the *hanhalah* and tried their best to convince them to change their minds. They discussed how all of Eliezer's brothers had done so well in the yeshivah, what a good boy Eliezer was, how supportive the parents were of the yeshivah through the years, and the excellent relationship they had with the *mosad.* However, they were up against a wall. The administrators maintained that they had picked up on something during the interview and gave the patented "We would be doing him a disservice if we accepted him" response.

Apparently, Hashem had an alternate plan for this boy.

It's not like there weren't any choices; there were many other options for a good *bachur* from a good *mishpachah* like Eliezer. But his path would not be the same as that of his brothers. Though his parents chose a very good yeshivah for him, it lacked the prestige and impressive size of his brothers' yeshivah. Theirs was a well-known institution of a thousand and Eliezer's was a no-name yeshivah with merely 150 students. Eliezer, who realized what he had lost, wasn't pacified by the pitch that a small *shiur* provides *talmidim* with more individualized attention. He preferred to be the tail of the lion than the head of a nice little rabbit. As much as he tried to convince himself, he was extremely bothered by the rejection and couldn't understand why this had to happen to him.

No matter what anyone told him, he was certain that settling on this yeshivah would prevent him from growing up like his brothers.

On the first day of the *zman*, Eliezer was taking a walk and trying to clear his mind when an older woman came over to him and asked if he was a *yeshivah bachur*. Although he wasn't an accomplished *talmid chacham* after one day in *yeshivah gedolah,* he was most certainly a *yeshivah bachur,* so he responded in the affirmative.

"My name is Geveret Hildenberg, and I'm looking for someone to give a weekly *Pirkei Avos shiur* in my home," the woman explained sincerely. "Would you be willing to give it every Shabbos?"

After thinking for a minute, Eliezer decided, *Why not?* He discussed the opportunity with his rebbeim, who encouraged him to go ahead, and so it began. Eliezer prepared well every week, and every Shabbos afternoon, a group of older men came to Geveret Hildenberg's house. Each week, he expounded on the theme of one Mishnah, adding in some stories, and the men found the *shiur* extremely interesting and inspiring. They loved the intimate setting and the humble manner of the *maggid shiur*. When the *shiur* was over, they enjoyed the repast — the cake and beverages Geveret Hildenberg provided — and the opportunity to schmooze with one another.

After a few years, they finished *Pirkei Avos* and Eliezer began to give a *shiur* in *Navi* with a similar style. Before the Yamim Tovim, he would give a special seasonal *shiur*. Week after week, Eliezer gave it his all. Geveret Hildenberg, who had never married and lived alone, always expressed her appreciation. This went on for several very enjoyable years.

In due time, the phone calls started coming in; Eliezer was of marriageable age. Although his brothers had received the most prestigious *shidduch* offers, Eliezer's, while respectable, always had a "but" attached to the suggestion. It's not that these young ladies were of any less quality, but their families were generally of minimal means.

After a few weeks, Eliezer's parents chose the girl they felt best suited their son. An outstanding girl — she was supportive, sensitive, and vivacious and would be the ideal wife for Eliezer.

But — there was absolutely no money.

Nada.

Nothing.

It meant that Eliezer and his *kallah* would probably not be able to live near their parents; they could only afford an apartment outside of Yerushalayim, if that. Nonetheless, everything else lined up and the two began meeting. A few weeks later, they were engaged.

Now, the financial worries became a little more realistic. Though Eliezer was very happy with his *kallah,* he would have to find a place to live and figure out how to pay their bills. The thoughts of his lack of acceptance into *yeshivah gedolah* and accompanying paranoia crept once more into his mind. He loved his yeshivah and had experienced huge success. He had blossomed into an excellent *bachur*. Nevertheless, the nagging doubt would not leave him. *Why me? Why did my path have to be different?*

Shaking off the feelings of uncertainty, he strengthened himself once more, as he had always tried to do when these feelings surfaced. He worked on his *emunah* and *bitachon* and contemplated the endless goodness in his life.

One day, he received a phone call. It was Geveret Hildenberg. Over the years, he had developed a very warm relationship with her. She was old enough to be his grandmother and she always expressed such gratitude for what he had done. Now she was calling because she had something to tell him, and asked him to come over so she could speak to him in person.

Never in a million years could he have imagined what she wanted to say.

Eliezer knocked on the door and was invited into the apartment where he had spent every Shabbos afternoon for so many years. For the first minute or so, Geveret Hildenberg fumbled for words. Then it came out. "What I am about to tell you is going to shock you. My father was a horrible person, a Nazi who murdered Jews during the Holocaust."

Eliezer sat in stunned silence. What had she just said?! He couldn't help wondering if this was just a nightmare. Squirming in his seat, he began thinking of a way to excuse himself. However, she was crying and anxious to share her story. "I was born after the war and when I discovered what my father had done, I was revolted by his past. I began searching and learning more and more about the people he had tried to exterminate. Though my family was extremely wealthy, I chose to leave my home and convert. I took some of the money and I fled my blood-soaked country and came to Eretz Yisrael, where I purchased this four-bedroom apartment, right here in Yerushalayim. I was so filled with shame that I could never bring myself to marry. I just wanted to spend my life seeking atonement for the sins of my father.

"I was thinking about whom to give my apartment to. All these years, you filled my home with the sweet sounds of Torah. You never asked for money and I never offered it. Now I want you to have my apartment; that would make me the happiest person in the world. I've already had the papers drawn up by a lawyer. The apartment is worth a lot of money and you will be able to raise a family here. I don't know what your plans were, but I hope this can help in some small way."

Eliezer tried to process what she was saying. It was all too much. Though he wanted to discuss it further, Geveret Hildenberg was emotionally drained and told him to think it over and let her know at a later date. Eliezer offered his heartfelt thanks and left.

Immediately, he ran to the Kosel HaMaaravi, where he threw himself onto the sacred stones and spoke directly to Hashem. "*Ribbono Shel Olam*, please forgive me. Until now, I wondered why You made life so difficult for me, why was I the only one in the family who had to go to a different yeshivah. Now I understand.

You wanted to reward me. You wanted me to deliver *shiurim* and be *mechazek* other Yidden. You wanted me to help Geveret Hildenberg find redemption. Now I got the best of everything. I could never have imagined that this was Your plan. Please forgive me for ever asking questions."

A few weeks later, the papers were signed. Geveret Hildenberg asked Eliezer to be discreet so the story would not get out.

Today, Eliezer is a rav with a beautiful family.

Living in a spacious apartment with children and grandchildren — and the light of Torah to illuminate their home.

It often happens that if we allow Hashem's plan to take hold, we are zocheh to watch the berachah unfold before our very eyes.

Our Every Move

Sometimes we make the mistake of thinking that great people have it easy. We fail to recognize that they, too, experience pivotal moments where their future hangs in the balance. One such individual was Aryeh. Here is his story in his own words.

WHEN I WAS 16 AND LEARNING IN YESHIVAS SLABODKA in the early 1950s, I was not deriving much satisfaction from my learning. My father found some older boys to learn with me for both first and second *seder*. While that helped for a short time, one of my *chavrusos* soon left the yeshivah, and the young man who took his place was not a good match for me.

Unfortunately, some of my friends also began to lose hope in me. They sensed that I didn't share their aspirations. I insisted that I wanted it to happen, I wanted to learn well, but it wasn't like I could just snap my fingers and feel fulfilled. Before long, they dropped me.

That Sivan, right in middle of the *zman,* I began to look for a new yeshivah. One day, I picked myself up and went to see Rav Moshe Shmuel Shapiro, the rosh yeshivah in Yeshivas Be'er Yaakov at the time. I told him about my situation, asked if I could switch to his yeshivah, and named the *shiur* I wanted to become part of: the third-level *shiur*. At first, he was hesitant. I was much younger than the rest of the boys in the third-year *shiur*. But since I was on the tall side and looked a little bit older than I was, he agreed to let me join.

Growing up in my parents' home, I had gleaned a great deal of guidance about navigating life's experiences, one of which is not to make a major decision without first asking advice from a *talmid chacham. Emunas chachamim* was paramount. I had gone to the Chazon Ish for guidance from the time I was 6 years old, and I considered him my rebbi already then. Although he wasn't feeling well when I came to discuss my idea, he agreed to speak to me. I shared my plan, but when I told him I was going to join the third-year *shiur*, he questioned me. He felt that since I was not that advanced in learning, I would be better off in the first-year *shiur*. He didn't want me to feel inadequate. Upon hearing his concerns, I acquiesced. I would join Yeshivas Be'er Yaakov, and attend the first-year *shiur.*

I left his house and went straight home. When I arrived, I saw my parents standing in the entranceway, waiting for me. They asked me where I had been and I told them that I had gone to speak with the Chazon Ish, detailing my plan to switch yeshivos, my visit to Rav Shapiro, and the advice the Chazon Ish had given me.

My parents couldn't believe it. Who just picks up and leaves in middle of a *zman*?

They went back to the Chazon Ish. Although he had heard my

side of the story, when he learned of my parents' opposition, the Chazon Ish retracted his decision, and concluded that I could not switch — not without my parents' approval. I would have to wait until the Elul *zman* to make the switch.

I was completely broken. It wasn't like I had just decided everything on my own. I had gone through the proper channels and discussed it with my rebbi, the *gadol hador*. Now that I was prevented from going, I had a real dilemma on my hands. I *couldn't* go to Be'er Yaakov, but I *wouldn't* go back to Slabodka, the yeshivah I had been planning on leaving.

Walking past the Heiligman Shul on Rechov Rabbi Akiva, I decided to pop in there and sit down and learn. I would make this my own place, my own yeshivah. As a teenager, I believed I could do anything. With no one there from morning until evening, I would be able to learn in peace and quiet until Elul, when I would go to Be'er Yaakov.

I opened a Gemara and sat down to learn. A few minutes later, an unexpected guest arrived: Rav Elazar Tzadok Turchin, the well-known *talmid chacham* and *marbitz Torah,* who was a *talmid* of Rav Shimon Shkop, the Chazon Ish, and the Brisker Rav. He must have seen me sitting alone, because he asked me if I wanted to learn with him *Maseches Beitzah*: Gemara, Rashi, and Tosafos. It's not like my schedule was full, so I took him up on his offer. I learned with him every day for four to six hours, from Sivan until Elul.

The learning finally became sweet to me.

Additionally, I learned *Maseches Shabbos* with Rav Moshe Yehoshua Landau, another *talmid* of the Chazon Ish. He helped me delve deeper into the *sugya,* and he also helped me appreciate the privilege of *limud Torah.*

Everything was working out just perfectly.

But the *yetzer hara* unleashed a ferocious attack against my still vulnerable *neshamah.* Although I had begun to taste success in my learning, I was still a relative novice. That Yom Kippur night, thoughts of doubt and discontent flooded my mind and my heart, causing me to question if I was making the right choice by remaining in yeshivah. Maybe the time had come for me to give it all up? After all, not everyone is cut out for learning, and I was still way behind many of my former friends.

I cried and fought with my *yetzer hara* all night long. I recited the entire *Sefer Tehillim,* finishing just before daybreak.

Finally, I felt I had made it. The tears had given me the strength to break through.

A short while later, I went to visit the Chazon Ish, to help him out since he was very weak, and also to update him on my situation. But when I knocked on the door, there was no answer. Concerned that perhaps the Chazon Ish was in danger, I kept knocking, harder and harder. When there was still no answer, I went around to the front of the apartment and found the Chazon Ish resting on the porch. Though his eyes were closed, when he sensed I was standing a mere few feet from him, he stirred and opened his eyes. "Aryeh? Is that you?"

"Yes," I responded. "What can I do for the rav?"

"Climb over the fence."

I quickly removed my hat and jacket. Knowing I would need them later, though, I began to scale the fence with the hat and jacket in my hands. Soon enough, the task proved too difficult, especially with so much in my hands, and the jacket fell to the ground. Next came the hat. Finally, I myself slipped off the bars and fell backward, and the next thing I knew I was lying on the ground. Aware that my rebbi really needed me, I quickly stood up and dusted myself off. Then I tried to climb the fence once more, placing one hand on an iron bar while grabbing hold of the next one. In this way, I made a little bit of headway but before I got too high, I fell to the ground once again. My frustration mounted as I continued. With each endeavor, I managed to reach a bit higher — but then fell to the ground. After the fourth attempt, I was just about ready to give up. I had tried my best, yet it just wasn't meant to be. Someone else would have to come help the Chazon Ish.

However, as I prepared to walk away, I looked at the Chazon Ish once more, and I grasped that with his failing health, it was just a matter of time before I would no longer have the chance to care for him or speak to him. So I mustered my strength and once again began the task of climbing the fence. Finally, on the fifth try, I made it all the way.

Now I was standing face-to-face with the Chazon Ish. I was exhausted and my hands hurt. My jacket and pants were filthy and my hat was smashed. But it was worth it; there was no longer a fence separating me from my rebbi.

The Chazon Ish pulled me close with his frail hands and told me something very important. "Aryeh, keep climbing. No matter what happens, no matter how difficult it may be, continue to climb. You may fall time and again. But pick yourself up, dust yourself off, and keep on climbing."

These were the last words the Chazon Ish shared with me — and I would never forget them. He understood my struggles and appreciated how far I had come.

Aryeh eventually became Rav (Yehuda) Aryeh Schechter, a disciple not only of the Chazon Ish, but also the Brisker Rav and other Torah giants. A big talmid chacham, Rav Aryeh was also a featured lecturer for Arachim and other outreach organizations, and was instrumental in helping bring back thousands to the proper path of Torah.

It seems surprising that he had his share of precarious moments. But he did, and he would frequently tell his story, a story that never fails to inspire.

Let's hear the end of his story, again in his words.

I continued to learn with Rav Moshe Yehoshua Landau, and always expressed my appreciation for what he had done for me and my learning. But I did not keep up with Rav Elazar Tzadok Turchin.

About 40 years after my initial *chavrusashaft* with Rav Turchin,

I reminisced about my youth and made the decision to go back to Bnei Brak. I wanted to visit Rav Turchin and thank him for turning my life around. Where would I be without his timely offer to learn with me in the Heiligman Shul?

Before setting out to Bnei Brak, I stopped in the Zichron Moshe "*shtieblach*" to daven Minchah. And whom should I meet, but Rav Elazar Tzadok, who had also come there to daven! What were the chances?

As I expressed my wholehearted appreciation to Rav Elazar Tzadok and I revealed to him what I had gone through earlier that day decades earlier, Rav Elazar Tzadok stopped me mid-sentence. "And who do you think told me to go there and learn with you? It was the Chazon Ish! I went to visit him and he told me, 'Aryeh is in Heiligman's Shul. Go there and learn with him!'"

But how had the Chazon Ish known?

That, no one will ever know.

The gadol hador anticipated the next move of a struggling teenager. And with sensitivity and insight, he turned his life around.

So many lessons can be learned from this story. Perhaps the most important lesson of all is that we must recognize that if the gadol hador anticipates our moves and watches over us and guides us, all the more so is Hashem keeping a watchful eye on us.

We must always remember how the Al-mighty watches our every step and our every move.

Whether we know it or not.

The King's Bar Mitzvah

No matter who we are and in which era we live, as Jews, we are an inseparable part of Hashem and His Torah. Rabbi Yehoshua Michaeli, the gabbai in Kollel Bnei Torah of Lakewood, shared an experience that speaks to the core of this message.

A FEW YEARS AGO, THE RAV OF THE SHUL, RAV AVRAHAM Lefkowitz, called Reb Yehoshua on Erev Shabbos of *Parashas Lech Lecha* and told him he would be away for Shabbos, and reminded him that their shul was hosting the Ohr Somayach Shabbaton that week. In order to give the Ohr Somayach boys a taste of Lakewood and frum life, the yeshivah placed the boys in homes around the neighborhoods near Beth Medrash Govoha. On Friday, they'd visit BMG and meet the roshei yeshivah, and on Motza'ei Shabbos, the yeshivah would throw a gala Melaveh Malkah for them. That year, the Shabbos *tefillos* were to take place in Kollel Bnei Torah.

On Shabbos morning, as Shacharis was about to begin, the local organizer of the Shabbaton approached Reb Yehoshua and said, "Though he is already in his early 20s, one of our boys never had a bar mitzvah, so we'll be celebrating his bar mitzvah this Shabbos!" Reb Yehoshua appreciated the heads-up and looked forward to participating in this special event, enhancing an already special Shabbos.

But he wondered which *aliyah* to give this young man. A bar mitzvah boy customarily receives the *aliyah* of *maftir*. In this instance, though, the boy was a beginner and could hardly read Hebrew. Furthermore, he wasn't *leining,* so there was no specific need to give him that *aliyah*.

Additionally, a grandfather or a close relative is usually honored with the *aliyah* preceding the bar mitzvah, so he can stand at the *bimah* and *schep nachas* as the bar mitzvah boy receives his first *aliyah*. This boy's father was not present, nor was any other relative. However, Rav Nota Schiller, rosh yeshivah of Ohr Somayach, was his mentor and leader of the program, and Chazal say, "*Kol ha'melamed es ben chaveiro Torah maaleh alav ha'kasuv ke'ilu yelado* — Whoever teaches his friend's son Torah, the Torah views him as if he had fathered him" (Rashi, *Bamidbar* 3:1; *Sanhedrin* 19b). With that in mind, Reb Yehoshua decided to give the bar mitzvah boy the *aliyah* following Rav Schiller. As a rosh yeshivah, Rav Schiller would be receiving the prestigious *aliyah* of *shelishi,* and the bar mitzvah boy would thus be called up for *revi'i*.

After the *chazzan* finished *Chazaras HaShatz* for Shacharis, Reb Yehoshua asked the organizer for the boy's Hebrew name. He replied, "Melech ben Yaakov." Reb Yehoshua had never heard of the name Melech, but the organizer confirmed it was his name.

Rav Schiller finished the *berachah* and Reb Yehoshua called up the *bachur*: "*Yaaaamod! Habachur habar mitzvah, Melech ben Yaakov, revi'i chazak*!" Hair to his shoulders, yarmulke perched precariously on his head, the boy strode to the *bimah* and somehow eked out the *berachah.*

Then the *leining* began:

בִּימֵי אַמְרָפֶל **מֶלֶךְ** שִׁנְעָר אַרְיוֹךְ **מֶלֶךְ** אֶלָּסָר כְּדָרְלָעֹמֶר **מֶלֶךְ** עֵילָם וְתִדְעָל. . . **מֶלֶךְ** גּוֹיִם: עָשׂוּ מִלְחָמָה אֶת בֶּרַע **מֶלֶךְ** סְדֹם וְאֶת בִּרְשַׁע **מֶלֶךְ** עֲמֹרָה שִׁנְאָב **מֶלֶךְ** אַדְמָה וְשֶׁמְאֵבֶר **מֶלֶךְ** צְבֹיִים **וּמֶלֶךְ** בֶּלַע. . .

As the *baal korei* continued, Reb Yehoshua was struck by the number of times the Torah mentions the word מֶלֶךְ in its description of the war of the four kings versus the five kings. After the *leining,* he counted carefully and came up with the number 21! He said to himself, "Here I just called up this bar mitzvah boy named Melech for this *aliyah,* and the Torah is basically calling his name, over and over again!"

When davening ended and the *Kiddush* began, Reb Yehoshua

went over to the boy and asked him his age. To his astonishment, Melech replied that he was 21 years old, equivalent to the number of times the word מֶלֶךְ appeared in that *aliyah*! After calling for everyone's attention, Reb Yehoshua related the story to all those present, who were astonished as he. Seeing their reaction, he turned to the young man. "Melech, it's your bar mitzvah today! You thought you were late in the game, but you see that the Torah itself is calling out to you: 'Melech!' So don't lose your fire and determination. Make Hashem and all of us proud!" What a special moment it was.

Two years later, Reb Yehoshua was walking in Flatbush one Shabbos, when he saw none other than Melech walking toward him. At first, Melech didn't recognize Reb Yehoshua, but when Reb Yehoshua reminded him of *Parashas Lech Lecha* in Lakewood, he remembered the event.

In truth, it was very surprising that Reb Yehoshua recognized Melech. After all, now he was dressed like a *yeshivah bachur*, walking with friends, and smiling widely. They spoke for a few minutes and he let Reb Yehoshua know that he was learning in *beis midrash* full time.

A true "*ben Melech*."

We say daily in davening (U'Va Le'Tzion), "Ve'chayei olam nata be'socheinu — And He implanted within us eternal life." Each of us can find ourselves planted right there in the Torah.

We just have to remain on the lookout!

All Taken Care Of

ILAN, A SECULAR TEENAGER, GREW UP ON THE CAREFREE streets of Haifa, and was raised by a father who never missed an opportunity to make a snide remark about the *chareidim*. One day, Ilan saw a sign plastered on the wall advertising an exciting *shiur*. Despite his father's constant comments, Ilan himself didn't dislike the religious way of life; he just knew practically nothing about it. When he first saw the sign, he felt drawn to the event. When he perused it more carefully, he noticed that prizes were being distributed, and that clinched it. Never one to deny himself a freebie, Ilan resolved that the next Monday he would be in attendance.

Ilan enjoyed the *shiur* very much. By the time it was over, he wasn't even thinking about the prizes; he just wanted to know when the next one was scheduled. He had really connected with the teacher and was inspired by the content. His father's reaction to his going to a *shiur* would not be pleasant, so he didn't plan on telling him. He went a few more times and enjoyed himself more and more every time. Soon enough, he was pining to go to yeshivah.

At that point, he realized it was time to come clean with his father. Upon hearing his wishes, his father became furious and lashed out at Ilan. "The day you walk into a yeshivah will be the day you never enter this house again!" The comment stung deeply. He had never seen his father display such anger. What could be so bad about learning Torah? Ilan spoke to his mother, who was more understanding, but every time he tried to bring up the topic again with his father, he refused to speak about it and warned Ilan repeatedly that he better not go.

After much thought, Ilan decided that he owed it to himself to discover the truth and to pursue it. He couldn't allow whatever was bothering his father to hold him back. One of his new mentors recommended a small yeshivah up north and he registered there and left his home. Before long, Ilan, who was a very bright young man, was catching up on his learning and making notable strides. The rosh yeshivah loved him and his rebbi took a strong personal interest in him, opening his home and his heart to the thirsty newcomer. Every Shabbos, Ilan ate at the home of a different member of the *hanhalah* and he spent Yom Tov at his rosh yeshivah's home.

Not only that, but his rebbi told Ilan that whenever he needed money, he would be happy to provide the necessary funds. Although this was a very kind gesture, Ilan still felt embarrassed that he had no money of his own. And as much as he tried to push it aside, the shame continued to gnaw at him. He knew his rebbi had a large family and that any money spent on him would take away from the rebbi's family's needs.

One night, Ilan went into the empty *beis midrash,* opened the *aron kodesh,* and cried for help. "*Ribbono Shel Olam*, I accept upon myself to finish the entire Shas within three years, but I need Your help to do it. I need You to provide me with the necessary peace of mind so I can fulfill my promise. I can't live without money. I need to know that if I want to buy some food or clothing or a *sefer,* I will be able to. To rely on others causes me too much shame. Please, I beg You, help me!"

Two days later, Ilan was walking down the street when he noticed a bag on the floor. He walked over and looked inside. The bag contained 20,000 shekel! He picked up the money and ran to a rav and asked what to do. The rav told him, "In this city, there are many non-Jewish people, including Arabs. Additionally, there are a lot of Jewish people who are not Torah observant. Therefore, anyone who loses money is going to give up hope, assuming that whoever finds it is not interested in returning it. You can keep the money."

It was an extremely quick response to Ilan's heartfelt cry. Now he would have peace of mind. With newfound vigor, he immersed himself in his learning, and, true to his commitment, made a Siyum HaShas at the end of three years.

By now, the time had come for Ilan to start looking for a wife. But it would not be so simple. Although he was an excellent *bachur*, many people would not be interested in a young man without a supportive family. This was especially true because his father was so antagonistic.

One day, one of the yeshivah's supporters, Reb Yaakov, came to the yeshivah looking for a *shidduch* for his daughter, and the rosh yeshivah recommended Ilan. He was upfront about the family situation, but maintained that there was no better boy in the yeshivah. Reb Yaakov met Ilan and he liked him right away. He asked the rosh yeshivah to arrange the *shidduch* and a few weeks later, Ilan was engaged to Reb Yaakov's daughter.

It was a huge *simchah* in the yeshivah. Ilan had come so far in such a short time, and developed into such an outstanding young man. He deserved this opportunity, and everybody rejoiced with him.

After the *l'chaim,* Reb Yaakov sat down with his son-in-law and began schmoozing about how Ilan had managed to finish Shas. Reb Yaakov didn't want to pry or get too personal; he was just interested to know how Ilan had been able to set such a goal for himself and reach it.

Ilan told his father-in-law about his journey from Haifa, and how at one point he almost fell apart. He told him about his intense moment when he stood in front of the *aron kodesh,* the deal he made with the *Ribbono Shel Olam,* and the money he'd found just two days later.

And then he looked up at his future father-in law.

Whose jaw had dropped.

Reb Yaakov asked when and where the money was found, and Ilan identified the date and precise location. Reb Yaakov realized that that was where he himself had lost 20,000 shekels; Ilan had found his future father-in-law's bag of money! And, as the rav had explained, Reb Yaakov had immediately given up hope of ever finding it again.

With tears in his eyes, Reb Yaakov began to laugh. He remembered the day well, how he'd felt when he had lost the money, how dejected he was. Little did he know that the money was going to help support his future son-in-law and help him develop into the *talmid chacham* he was meant to be.

How wondrous are the ways of Hashem!

Stunning Salvation

DURING THE PERIOD OF THE BRITISH MANDATE, THOUGH there was an overwhelming amount of interest among Jews to settle in "Palestine" in order to escape the European inferno, very few were able to gain entry. Only those with some sort of a "connection" were able to secure a visa to Eretz Yisrael. When Rav Isser Zalman Meltzer was still in Europe, three of his *talmidim* asked him to write a letter on their behalf to the chief rabbi, Rav Yitzchak Isaac Herzog, urging him to use his connections with the government to help them obtain visas.

As Rav Isser Zalman was writing the letter, he listed the boys' names. For some reason, he wrote Yitzchak Epstein first, though Yitzchak was the last of the three to make the request. Recognizing that the names should be listed in the order that the requests had been placed, Rav Isser Zalman tore up the first draft of his letter and took out another paper with which to write another one.

Strangely, though, when he wrote the second letter, he repeated his mistake and again wrote Yitzchak Epstein's name in front of the other two. Intrigued by the odd occurrence, Rav Isser Zalman remembered a *kabbalah* from the Chofetz Chaim that someone of a clear mind doesn't make the same mistake twice. "So if I made the same mistake two times consecutively, it must be *retzon Hashem*." As such, he decided to leave it as is, and he sent the letter requesting the visas with the name of Yitzchak Epstein preceding the other two names.

A few weeks later, he received a response. Rav Herzog apologized, stating that the certificates were almost impossible to come by, and he wasn't able to secure three of them, only one. And he chose the first name on the list, Yitzchak Epstein, to receive the visa.

Upon reading the letter, Rav Isser Zalman was taken by the *hashgachah pratis*. He never intended for Yitzchak to be the first. On two separate occasions, he inadvertently wrote his name first. Obviously, for reasons only known to Hashem, Yitzchak was meant to obtain a visa.

Yitzchak made his way to Eretz Yisrael. When Rav Isser Zalman arrived a while later, Yitzchak maintained a very close connection with him and was intimately involved in the publication of Rav Isser Zalman's magnum opus, *Even HaAzel*, a compilation of his *chiddushim*.

During the Israeli War of Independence, as the Jordanians pummeled Yerushalayim with relentless shelling, a grenade exploded right near the home of Rav Isser Zalman. Shrapnel ripped into his leg, causing him to lose a dangerous amount of blood. Rebbetzin Baila Hinda cried out for help and immediately, a *talmid* who was nearby came running to Rav Isser Zalman's side. But Rav Isser Zalman whispered in his ear, "If people hear I was hit, they will come to help me despite the danger. I'd rather leave this world than have others risk their own lives to save me."

The *talmid* refused to listen to his request. Under a storm and barrage of explosions, he ran outside to cry for help, when he saw an army ambulance passing by. Standing in middle of the road, he pleaded with the driver to stop. "Someone inside this house is badly wounded. He must go to the hospital immediately, or he will die!"

The driver of the ambulance was not moved. "People are wounded all over the city. I want to take everyone. I'm sorry, but it's forbidden to transport civilians; I am only allowed to take soldiers. Please get out of the way and allow us to do what we have to do."

The *talmid* would not budge. Frantically, he demanded, "The wounded individual is Rav Isser Zalman Meltzer! He's losing blood as we speak. You must take him to the hospital right now!"

When the driver heard Rav Isser Zalman's name, he agreed to transport him, though he understood he may be court-martialed for it. The *talmid* brought Rav Isser Zalman into the ambulance and jumped into the seat next to him. As soon as he arrived at the hospital, Rav Isser Zalman was treated and his life was saved. The doctors told him that if he would have arrived two minutes later, he would have died from the enormous amount of blood lost.

However, the wound soon developed an infection and again the doctors feared for his life. After that crisis passed, he was brought to the home of his daughter and son-in-law in Petach Tikva, and the *bachurim* of Lomza Yeshivah took care of him and changed his bandages twice daily. Ultimately, despite his brush with death, Rav Isser Zalman was nursed back to health, and he continued to be *marbitz Torah* for many years.

Who was this bachur who fought so hard to save Rav Isser Zalman's life?

It was Yitzchak Epstein, to whom Rav Isser Zalman had given a ticket to life.

Now he reciprocated his rebbi's favor by saving his.

Swimming to Survive

It's a highly unlikely story. Few could have predicted its outcome. But much like the story of the Jewish people, the heroes of this story overcame enormous adversity to not only survive, but to shine in ways never imagined.

RAV SHMUEL AND REBBETZIN RIVKAH WOSNER WERE married for just a short while when the storms of war began to threaten Vienna, where they first set up their home. Rav Shmuel heard the rumors and paid close attention to the terrifying news of Hitler's activities. Then one day, after receiving a tongue lashing from some anti-Semitic Austrians, Rav Shmuel told his wife it was time to leave.

They went to share the news with the rebbetzin's parents, people of means, explaining that they feared the imminent destruction and felt it was time to go, to move to Eretz Yisrael. At the time, the British, who were in control of Palestine, denied entry to anyone who did not have proper papers, which were difficult to obtain.

Rav Shmuel's father-in-law did not agree with their plans, maintaining that it was dangerous to travel to Eretz Yisrael; it was wiser, he felt, to wait until the storm passed. Rav Shmuel countered that staying was even more dangerous. Ultimately, they agreed to ask a *shailah* from a rav in nearby Bratislava (Pressburg). The rav *paskened* that it was better to leave and go to Eretz Yisrael.

After researching their options, Rav Shmuel discovered that although they were unable to secure the needed legal documents, there was an illegal boat with space, whose captain was willing to take them. Food was scarce on the ship and the accommodations awful, yet there was a much more pressing issue. What would the rav and rebbetzin do with their toddler, Chaim Meir, who was only a year and a half old?

They decided to leave Chaim Meir with Rebbetzin Rivkah's parents. Once the Wosners were settled in Eretz Yisrael, they would arrange for the baby to be brought over. No one could have imagined that the situation would deteriorate so rapidly and to such an extent, and it would be years until they saw him again.

Rav and Rebbetzin Wosner boarded the ship and after a tearful goodbye, set sail. The British knew how frantic the Jews were to leave Europe. Yet instead of showing compassion, they doubled their efforts to prevent any such ships from reaching land. If a ship attempted to approach the shores of Palestine without permission, the British treated it as an enemy ship and attacked.

As the Wosners' ship neared Eretz Yisrael, the captain did his best to stay far away from British eyes, hoping to elude the authorities, but soon he couldn't wait anymore; the ship had run out of fuel. Now they were stranded two kilometers off the coast of Netanya. The captain gathered the exhausted passengers and spelled out their two options. They could either stay on the ship and hope that somehow they would be saved, or they could jump off the ship and swim to shore.

It was the second night of Chanukah, the middle of December, in the pitch blackness of night; the water was freezing. The chances of survival were slim at best. But staying on the boat didn't seem the better option. A group of fourteen (out of about one hundred and fifty) jumped into the water.

Rav Shmuel and Rebbetzin Rivkah, though, did not join them. Swimming with the others constituted a lack of *tznius*. Instead, they took a circuitous — obviously longer and more precarious — route through the icy waters to the shore. Both excellent swimmers, after hours of swimming through the frigid sea, Rav Shmuel and his rebbetzin reached the shore. In all, only four other passengers survived. The others drowned not far from freedom.

When they arrived, utterly exhausted and frozen from their

harrowing journey, Rav Shmuel and Rebbetzin Rivkah found a door with a *mezuzah* and knocked. The fellow who answered the door grew frightened when he saw the ragtag pair and slammed the door. Despite his fatigue, Rav Shmuel would not give up. Their clothes were drenched, stuck to their skin. More than anything, his sense of *tznius* and propriety drove him to find respectable clothing. The residents of the next house were more welcoming and more accommodating. The man of the house allowed them to enter and offered them a change of garments, some warm food and drink, and some money; all their valuables had fallen into the sea.

Before long, Rav Shmuel was giving *shiurim* to *talmidei chachamim* in Yerushalayim.

For many months, Rav Shmuel and his rebbetzin did not receive any updates on their child, left on a burning continent. They heard rumors that millions were being killed, and they wondered: What were the chances that little Chaim Meir was still alive? With tensions so high, the rebbetzin's blood pressure often climbed to dangerous levels, confining her to bed for months at a time. Yet despite caring for his wife and agonizing over his child, Rav Wosner used every spare moment — and then some — to learn. He immersed himself in his *sefarim* day and night, as if his whole family were with him in Eretz Yisrael and all was peaceful.

Finally, the war ended and Rav Shmuel and Rebbetzin Rivkah received the wonderful news that Chaim Meir had survived and was safe in England. When they heard how he'd survived, the news nearly took their breath away. Rebbetzin Rivkah's wealthy parents had paid handsomely for a non-Jewish couple to take in Chaim Meir, which they did, together with another child. But one day, the Nazis received a tip that this non-Jewish couple was hiding Jewish children. When they came to the door and demanded the truth, the woman refused to acknowledge it. They threatened to kill her husband, but she still refused to give up the two children.

They shot her husband on the spot.

This righteous woman, from the *chassidei umos ha'olam,* continued to care for Chaim Meir Wosner as if he were her own.

Every year, on the second night of Chanukah, Rav Shmuel recounted this miraculous tale.

Yet another brilliant chapter of Jewish survival in the face of bitter darkness. With the support of his rebbetzin, Rav Shmuel, the author of the Shevet HaLevi, rosh yeshivah of Yeshivas Chachmei Lublin in Bnei Brak and posek hador, would become a light unto to his nation.

As would his children.

The flame blazes on.

CHINUCH

A Matter of Interpretation

A GERRER CHASSID IN PREWAR EUROPE, TULI DEVELoped a close rapport with his rebbeim, especially Rav Gad'l Eisner. Although his rebbeim made demands in terms of his *avodas Hashem*, Tuli felt deeply connected to them and embraced everything that was imparted to him. His davening was filled with vitality, excitement, and passion; he learned diligently, with much *hasmadah*.

But then, World War II began and everything was turned upside down.

Tuli lost his friends and his family.

He lost his community and almost all of his rebbeim.

Along the way, he lost his zest and spark for Yiddishkeit.

Adrift and angry, he abandoned the ways of old; Shabbos and kashrus fell by the wayside, and he removed his yarmulke, *tzitzis*, and any sign or vestige connecting him to Judaism.

Looking to start life anew, Tuli, or Thomas as he now called himself, began courting a non-Jewish girl. After a short while, they decided to get married.

Rachmana litzlan!

He didn't have to tell his parents (since they had been killed in the war), or anybody else, what he was about to do. After all, few people knew him. And even fewer seemed to care. It was tragic in so many ways.

There was only one person he wanted to tell. His rebbi. Though Thomas hadn't seen his rebbi in years, he still felt an urge to share the news with him. Maybe it was out of guilt, maybe he wanted to be talked out of it. Who knows? Regardless, he stopped by a yeshivah, reminiscent of the place where he had spent so much of his life before the war, a building where he had been at home, but where he now felt like an utter and complete stranger, perhaps even an enemy.

Feeling uneasy, he peeked into the building looking for his rebbi, Rav Gad'l Eisner. To any passerby, here was a curious non-Jew looking in. Nothing about his presence indicated otherwise.

Finally, Thomas built up the courage to walk inside and he soon spotted Rav Gad'l. "Can we talk?" Rav Gad'l quickly stood up and walked outside of the building. But Thomas wasn't ready to speak with him there. He asked if they could walk to a more discreet location, and the two continued walking until they reached the outskirts of town.

Thomas looked into Rav Gad'l's eyes and began to recount the horrific story of his last few years. He told him about all he'd lost. His family, friends, everything.

Rav Gad'l nodded empathetically. He knew the pain of loss. He, too, had lost his entire world.

Thomas continued to weave his story of woe and pain. Finally, he blurted, "I am going to marry a *shiksa*."

Rather than demonstrating horror, Rav Gad'l merely looked at his former *talmid*.

Uncomfortable with the silence, Thomas pressed on, "So what do you say, Rebbi?"

Now Rav Gad'l spoke. "To tell you the truth, it's been six years since I reviewed the halachos of *Even HaEzer* (the section of the *Shulchan Aruch* discussing family law such as marriage and divorce). But one thing I can tell you for sure. *Fahr ah Chassidishe bachur, es pas nisht!* For a Chassidishe boy, it's not befitting!"

Thick silence filled the air as Rav Gad'l's comment found its way into Thomas's heart. He had expected a thorough dressing-down, yet Rav Gad'l still referred to him as a *Chassidishe bachur.* And that meant everything to him.

Thomas began to turn his life around. The following day, he broke the news to his fiancée. He wasn't going to marry her.

Over the next few months, Thomas, now back to Tuli, slowly found his way home, eventually rebuilding his life.

Just the way Rav Gad'l wanted.

As a *Chassidishe yungerman.*

***

Rav Dovid Olewski, rosh yeshivah of the Gerrer Yeshivah in Boro Park, Brooklyn, shared another story about Rav Gad'l.

RAV GAD'L ONCE RECEIVED A MESSAGE FROM THE BEIS Yisrael, Rav Yisrael Alter of Ger, that a *bachur* in Yeshivas Chiddushei Harim in Tel Aviv, where Rav Gad'l served as mashgiach, had to be expelled from yeshivah.

When the Beis Yisrael issued a directive, he left no room for discussion. Nonetheless, a week later the boy was still in yeshivah.

Again, the Beis Yisrael sent a message to Rav Gad'l instructing him to throw the *bachur* out of yeshivah. And again, the boy remained.

A few weeks later, Rav Gad'l went to spend Shabbos with the Beis Yisrael in Yerushalayim and the Rebbe called him in. "I sent you a few messages to ask this boy to leave the yeshivah, and you didn't listen to me?"

Rav Gad'l responded, "I did listen to you."

"But I told you to send him out of the yeshivah."

"I did send him away."

"So he's not in yeshivah anymore?" asked the Rebbe.

"He is," replied Rav Gad'l.

The Rebbe questioned, "How can you say you told him to pack his bags if he's still in yeshivah?" It seemed so puzzling.

With great reverence, Rav Gad'l responded, "Regarding sending a *bachur* out, I hold like Rav Ashi in *Maseches Shabbos* 2b. '*Hachnasah nami hotza'ah kari lah* — Bringing in is also considered taking out.' In other words, my taking a boy in, meaning bringing him closer, is also a form of sending away." If one is *mekarev* a *bachur* and helps him straighten out, that can accomplish the same (or more) as showing him the door.

In a rare display of acquiescence, the Beis Yisrael accepted Rav Gad'l's reply and the *bachur* remained in yeshivah.

Once more, Rav Gad'l discovered the crack to enable a lost and forlorn boy to see the light again.

Giving the Grade

Some teachers have a one-size-fits-all grading system. Everyone is graded by how they do on the tests and everyone receives the same test. It doesn't matter how bright you are or what type of extenuating circumstances you may be working under. The grade is the grade. No negotiations.

But then there are teachers of a different sort, educators who understand that not every child can be graded with the same expectations. Hashem blessed each of us with varying levels of intellect. Some are smarter. Some more diligent. Some more studious.

And some less.

If a child is weaker, the rubric needs to change. Perhaps he is capable of answering only fifteen out of twenty questions on the test. That doesn't mean he gets a 75; rather, he is graded only on fifteen questions. If he gets fifteen right, then he receives his 100.

The Al-mighty, the Melamed Torah LeAmo Yisrael, understands that some children are smarter than others. In fact, He was the One Who made that determination. Some have been given the ability to sit for long periods of time while others struggle to sit for more than a half-hour.

Differentiated learning.

The Al-mighty understands His talmidim. He knows the challenge — and rewards accordingly.

THOUGH YANKY VERY MUCH WANTED TO SUCCEED, HE was not blessed with a good head for learning. No matter how hard he tried, he always found himself behind his peers. During his elementary school years, this was not so glaringly obvious, but as the years went by and the learning became more and more challenging, the gap between Yanky and his classmates grew. He worked hard and listened to *shiur* every day but failed to understand the material. There were times when he recorded the *shiur* and reviewed it again and again, yet still struggled to comprehend the *sugya*. He was only able to go so far, to dig so deep.

This made it difficult to find a *chavrusa*. No one wanted to learn with a boy who was so weak he couldn't understand the Gemara. Though his rebbeim managed to convince some of the stronger boys to learn with him, Yanky knew that nobody was doing so willingly, and it didn't do wonders for his self-esteem, confidence, or pride. Yanky felt like a failure. By the time he was 17, sadness and a deep, dark cloud of hopelessness engulfed him.

His rebbi tried to be *mechazek* him, to no avail. He told him all Hashem wants is for us to do our best, but Yanky wasn't convinced. Though he heard the words, they made little mark on his damaged psyche. Finally, his rebbi decided to take him to the Steipler Gaon, Rav Yaakov Yisrael Kanievsky. He didn't know what the Steipler would say, but he was confident that if anyone had the right words, it would be he.

As he presented his dilemma to the Steipler, Yanky's voice cracked from emotion. He detailed how because of his weak memory skills, he didn't have the background knowledge his friends had. Thus, he had to learn each Mishnah from scratch, with all of its references, as if he had never heard the concepts before. It took him months to learn what the other boys mastered in a few days. By the time he understood the first *daf*, the others in his *shiur* were eons ahead of him. While his peers were already on *daf yud* (page 10), he sadly conceded, "I'm only holding on *daf beis* (page 2, which is the first page)."

The Steipler, who was hard of hearing, asked him, "So you're holding on *daf kuf beis*, page 102?"

"No," Yanky corrected with reverence and respect, "*daf beis.*" But the Steipler repeated, "*Daf kuf beis*?"

Yanky didn't want to be disrespectful, but he was aware of the Steipler's hearing issues and he wanted the Steipler to understand clearly where his frustration lay. So he wrote down on a piece of paper in very clear letters, "*Higaati le'daf beis*, I reached page 2."

The Steipler looked at the vulnerable *bachur* and clarified, "*Bachur'l,* I heard you clearly. And I know that you think you got up to *daf beis*. But in *Shamayim,* they count differently. There you are up to *daf kuf beis*, because every *daf* you learn with difficulty is like 100 *dapim* to Hashem. Although you think you are ten *dapim* behind your friends, you are really ninety ahead of them! Do you still think you're unsuccessful? Do you still think you're behind in your learning?

"This is what we believe and you must believe it, as well. And if you do, you will feel so much more *berachah* in your learning, and you will feel so much happier and more satisfied."

Yanky walked away with a newfound belief in himself and went on to become quite accomplished in his learning.

Students often feel unsuccessful because they compare their accomplishments to the others in their class or shiur. Although it is always nice to grow together as a group, if the feelings of failure overwhelm you, then you must remember what really matters.

And Who is giving the grade.

The Bar Mitzvah Letter

WHEN AVRAHAM BORENSTEIN WAS BORN, THE ODDS were stacked against him. The year was 1971 and he and his parents lived in Communist Russia. At that time, the KGB stalked and tormented anyone whose life hinted at any religious practices. But Avraham's father was not afraid. He continued to do his utmost to live as a frum, practicing Jew. Even after the KGB had their eyes on him, he did not relent.

One day, they came.

Avraham was too young to remember, but his father was snatched away, taken to a labor camp in Siberia. Even there, he stubbornly refused to give up any of his Jewish practices, still keeping Shabbos and kosher. They tormented him and tortured him. Somewhere along the way, his body gave way.

Avraham would never see his father again.

Time went by and his mother did her best. Yet she was very limited. She tried to teach her son about being a Jew, but without a father it was very difficult. Aside from their religious struggles, there was another pressing challenge — they were destitute. They didn't have the means or the religious objects with which to perform mitzvos.

In the free world, when a Jewish boy celebrates his bar mitzvah, it is usually with friends and family. He wears his *tefillin* proudly; he is on his way to becoming a full-fledged *ben Torah*.

Avraham had none of that. On the night of his bar mitzvah, in their small, dark, and bare apartment, his mother gave him a gift. She sat him down and began to talk about his father, a fierce and courageous general. In the army of the Al-mighty.

She pulled out a Gemara, worn and weathered, its brittle pages torn from usage. "This was your father's Gemara! He fought to learn Torah."

Riveted, Avraham ran his hands over the delicate pages. His mother had never let the Gemara out of her bedroom; she didn't want anyone to see it and report her. But now, on this special night, she wanted to share it with her son. This was her gift — to tell her son about his father.

"Your father, the general, fought valiantly. He sacrificed his life and risked his freedom every day, fighting against the Communist forces that tried to eliminate the Al-mighty from our lives."

Then she disclosed what happened to his father. "He refused to violate the Shabbos. He wouldn't work on that sacred day. They beat him but he didn't give in. They wouldn't give him kosher food. Ultimately, they snuffed out his life. But always remember — he was a general!

"I was not able to give you so much Yiddishkeit. I didn't know how to teach you anything more than the basics. However, now that you are a bar mitzvah boy, I beg you to continue in the tradition of your father and your grandfather and all the generals from all the generations. Promise me that even if they take you away to Siberia and even if they torment you and torture you, you will continue to be a general until your very last breath."

As she spoke these words, she cried and he cried, as well. When she finally calmed down, she stood up and walked toward one of the cabinets. She opened it, pulled out an envelope, and handed it to him.

"Your father knew that one day he may be taken away, so he wrote this letter, an ethical will of sorts. As he wrote it, he, too, cried and cried. As you read, try to picture your father's emotions as he wrote it."

It was all so much to process. Avraham had always known his father was a *tzaddik* but the manner in which his mother spoke tonight, on the night of his bar mitzvah, made a huge impact on him.

He carefully opened the envelope and pulled out a piece of paper. Tears blurred his vision as he read.

Beni yakiri Avremel — My dear son Avremel,

I worry about you. I think about you all the time and I know no rest. What will be if they take me away? Who will raise you to be a good Yid? I know it's not easy to grow up without a father. But you should know that nobody is ever alone. You are always close to your Father in Heaven, and He will escort you every step of the way. Even in the frozen tundra of Russia, He will always be with you. And I will also be with you in spirit and soul. I will stand before the Heavenly Throne and beg the Al-mighty on your behalf.

You may wonder how I can do this. The answer is that a Yid who lives a life of Torah lives a life of angels. And an angel can never be killed. An angel continues to live on in Shamayim. Forever and ever.

We named you Avraham, hoping you would be like Avraham Avinu — you on one side of the world, fighting against the other side, the Communists, who deny the existence of Hashem.

We made your bris in secret and the Ribnitzer Rebbe served as the mohel. He shed many tears at your bris, infusing you with enormous siyata d'Shmaya, protecting your neshamah and keeping it holy.

The letter continued, with words of *emunah* and *chizuk,* advising Avraham that if he lives with the truth, he will be willing to die for it as well, just like his namesake, who was willing to be thrown into a fiery furnace. If someone is not willing to die for his cause, though, it's not worthwhile for him to live for it either. His father wrote about the story of Rabbi Akiva, who was willing to give up his life for Hashem.

Then he concluded:

One day, we will meet up again. You and I, and your grandfathers. Please promise me that when they meet you, they will be proud.

Mi'lev el lev — From heart to heart,
Abba

What a letter it was. As he grew older, Avraham read and reread those inspiring words, which drove him and motivated him to begin learning Torah.

But one question still bothered him. Even if he would do his utmost to live such a life, where would it take him? He was stuck in Russia. How could he grow in such a spiritually empty place? Could he ever get out?

When someone dreams the impossible dream, only the Almighty can make it happen. Avraham and his mother lived in a city called Chernobyl. On April 26, 1986, the reactor at the nuclear power plant at Chernobyl, Ukraine, went out of control, leading to an explosion and fire that demolished the reactor building, releasing large amounts of radiation into the atmosphere. All the people in the surrounding cities, 70,000 in all, had to be evacuated.

Avraham and his mother requested to go to Israel and inexplicably, were granted permission.

Today, Rav Avremshe Borenstein, a tzaddik and a talmid chacham, continues to make his father proud.

Money Well-Spent

Whenever young children would come to Rav Aharon Leib Shteinman for a bechinah, he made sure to ask them easy questions. He wasn't looking to stump them; he wanted to build them, to show them they were learning well, and to reward them with a berachah and a smile. A smile for which he was well-known, a smile that belied his greatness and instantly captured one's heart.

AN ENTHUSIASTIC REBBI BROUGHT HIS STUDENTS, WHO learned in a yeshivah in Central Israel, to Rav Aharon Leib's home in Bnei Brak for a *bechinah.* Before getting off the bus, the rebbi took the microphone and recited the first Mishnah in *Pirkei Avos* with his young charges, tracing our *mesorah* from Moshe Rabbeinu all the way back to the *Anshei Knesses HaGedolah.* Then he said to them, "Dear *kinderlach,* the Torah was given at Har Sinai, and was transmitted from one generation to the next through the *gedolei hador.* Now, with awe and reverence, we are going to enter our own small *maamad Har Sinai.*"

The atmosphere was charged with excitement as the boys entered the home of the venerated *gadol,* a strong feeling of *ahavas haTorah* suffusing the air. As Rav Aharon asked one very simple question after another, the boys answered confidently and he poured boundless praise upon their little heads. After each boy had successfully answered one question, he walked past Rav Aharon Leib, who shook each one's hand and gave each a *berachah.* They thanked Rav Aharon Leib and walked out of his apartment and down the steps. Then they hopped onto the bus that was waiting to take them and their *menahel* back to school in Central Israel.

After checking that all the stragglers had boarded the bus, the rebbi was ready to walk back to his house, which was in Bnei Brak. But then one of Rav Aharon Leib's *gabbaim* tapped him on the shoulder and asked him to please return; Rav Aharon Leib wanted to speak to him. With a touch of apprehension in his heart, he quickly turned around and ran back up the steps. Why did Rav Aharon Leib want a private audience with him? Had he not taught the material properly?

As soon as the rebbi walked in, Rav Aharon Leib put him at ease, praising him for choosing this lofty profession, and extolling the boys' *yiras Shamayim* and knowledge. The rebbi breathed a sigh of relief.

Rav Aharon Leib asked, "Who is traveling with the boys back to school?"

The rebbi replied, "The *menahel.*"

"Does your rebbetzin know you were here today?"

"Certainly."

"So she is waiting for you and you are delayed because of me."

"*Chalilah.*"

"There is a phone here. Please call her and tell her you will come home a little late because of me."

"Usually I come home much later, because I have to travel back from Central Israel."

"But today she is expecting you earlier because she knows you were here. It is forbidden to cause her even a second of worry."

"I'll call her."

After the phone call, Rav Aharon Leib expressed his appreciation. "Thank you for giving up your personal time for my sake." When the rebbi assured him that it was his *zechus* and his privilege, Rav Aharon Leib got down to business.

"I want to speak to you about two of the boys," and he identified them by the questions he had asked each one. When the rebbi acknowledged that he knew which boys he was referring to, Rav Aharon Leib stood up and walked into the other room, returning with 200 shekel, which he handed to the rebbi along with a request. "Please make sure to buy these two boys new shoes."

After the rebbi acquiesced, Rav Aharon Leib explained, "Don't think I have *ruach hakodesh* or anything. Generally, when little boys come to see me, a *Yehudi zakein,* an elderly Jew, their parents dress them in Shabbos clothes and Shabbos shoes. Nonetheless, I noticed that these two boys, even when dressed in their best, had torn shoes."

The rebbi was awestruck by the sensitivity and thoughtfulness. Hundreds of people walked past Rav Aharon Leib every day, yet he had taken the time to notice two little boys' torn shoes. He asked the sage, "How can one acquire this *middah* of being *nosei be'ol im chaveiro*?" Rav Aharon Leib emphasized to the rebbi the importance of taking note of every factor involving each of his *talmidim.* That is part of the responsibility of a rebbi and the only way to be a successful *mechanech.*

There was another boy on Rav Aharon Leib's roster, but before he addressed his concerns about that *talmid,* Rav Aharon Leib lowered his head and began to cry. "I'm already very old. I don't know what's going to be with me when I go to the Next World, what my judgment will be. I am very scared; I don't have many mitzvos to my name. So I need your help."

The rebbi was very confused. "The rosh yeshivah wrote the *sefer Ayeles HaShachar,* spread so much Torah and fear of Heaven, led the whole generation of Yidden..."

"I wish," replied Rav Aharon Leib. "Look, I am asking you for a favor, to help me in this area, and it will infringe on your personal time. Therefore, I would like to pay you each month, based on the time you invest and the rate you request. I hope to pay you in a timely manner as long as I remain in this world.

"When I asked one boy his question, I noticed he has a bad stutter. I can't begin to imagine how much shame and suffering it causes him. Therefore, I am asking you to never, ever ask him a question that he's going to have to answer in front of other people. Rather, tell him to stay after class and ask him the questions privately, so you can give him a proper test, either one-on-one or in writing. But do it in a way that nobody else will realize what you're doing. I will pay for the extra time it takes you."

The rebbi would not take any money for this, but he felt a pang. "Why didn't I think of this myself?" he cried.

Rav Aharon Leib specified how important it is for children to feel good about themselves and not be embarrassed. If a little boy sees that others care about him and take his needs seriously, he, too, will care for others and will become a *mentch.* And someone who is not a *mentch* cannot grow.

Here was someone who was holding much of the Torah world on his shoulders.

Yet that did not prevent him from carrying each individual child, as well.

For each one is so very precious.

The Kiss That Heals

WHEN ILAN HIGH SCHOOL FORMED IN DEAL, NEW JERsey, it was a game-changing moment for many of the students, the vast majority of whom came from non-observant homes. Nevertheless, their parents listened to their chachamim, who insisted that their daughters must learn Torah and that it cannot be taught in a coeducational setting; the classes must be separate. As such, a few dedicated Syrian lay leaders bankrolled the school and hired the very best teachers and educators to teach the girls, many of whom were none too pleased to be attending the school.

Most of them, in fact, were downright angry. They were not on board religiously, and socially the school constituted a tremendous inconvenience. Social setting is crucial to the daily life of teenagers, and to have that ripped away from them was devastating.

Sensing that leeway was needed, the administrators instructed the teachers that no matter how much a student misbehaved, she was not to be sent out of class. These girls were frustrated and upset and needed to express themselves. Throwing them out of a class they never wanted to be in in the first place would prove counterproductive.

Nevertheless, one day, early in the year, Mrs. Leah Trenk, the assistant principal, was sitting in her office when a 10th grader, Raquel, pranced in; it was clear she had been sent to the office by her teacher for misbehaving. Even though Raquel's teacher knew not to send out any of the girls, apparently Raquel had made it absolutely impossible to teach.

Mrs. Trenk, an experienced educator who lent her *chinuch* expertise and positivity to an already outstanding staff, was prepared for any eventuality. Looking to give the disruptive teenager a way out, Mrs. Trenk asked her if she was feeling all right. "You know, sometimes when people are not feeling well, they have a tendency to not act themselves. Maybe you acted out in class because you're sick?"

Although the suggestion was completely fabricated, and Raquel had never mentioned anything about not feeling well, she seemed willing to accept the excuse and possibly get out of trouble. Instead of using a thermometer, Mrs. Trenk made use of an age-old method of taking temperature. By placing one's lips on a child's forehead, in essence giving them a kiss, one can take their tactile temperature. This is precisely what Mrs. Trenk did to detect if Raquel was actually sick.

Of course, she wasn't.

Now Mrs. Trenk made her an offer she could not refuse. "How about you stay here in my office for a little bit and we talk? Maybe you will feel better. Then when you are ready, you can go back to class."

As they talked, it became clear why Raquel was particularly irate that day. Her parents were getting divorced. No wonder she was angry! As they spoke, Mrs. Trenk made Raquel feel welcome and loved. A while later, when she "felt better," Raquel returned to the classroom and her regular routine. But not before Mrs. Trenk proposed, "If you ever want to stop by and schmooze, feel free to do so. You are always welcome here."

At the time, Raquel was in 10th grade. From that day, until she graduated over two years later, Raquel would come to Mrs. Trenk's office to have "her temperature taken" and to schmooze.

Every.

Single.

Day.

Not surprisingly, Raquel, along with the majority of the other sullen students that first day, slowly became enveloped in the warmth and encouragement of Ilan's exceptional educators and began to embrace a Torah lifestyle.

Today, these women have been blessed with beautiful Torah families. Their bitterness is gone, replaced by an eagerness to give and to grow.

These students are often in touch with their high school teachers. Thankfully, they are "feeling fine," but who doesn't want to have their "temperature taken" every once in a while?

The Secret Holy Place

Though our homeland of Eretz Yisrael is inherently holy, everyone finds meaning in different places. Many find meaning while standing at the Kosel HaMaaravi; day or night you will find Yidden crying their hearts out at the Wall, reciting Tehillim, kissing its sacred stones. Others are moved when standing at the burial spot of our heilege Mamma, Kever Rachel, a place that brings our fragility and vulnerability to the fore. Or perhaps the awe, mystique, and reverence of Me'aras HaMachpeilah connect us to our Avos and Imahos, making praying there that much more significant. And yet, others connect to any one of the hundreds of kevarim of the tzaddikim buried throughout Eretz Yisrael.

Rav Moshe Halberstam had his own place to daven, a novel venue where he poured out his heart.

ONCE, AS RAV MOSHE AND HIS CHILDREN TRAVELED TO various *kevarim* in Eretz Yisrael, Rav Moshe asked the driver of the van to pull over and stop in the middle of what appeared to be "nowhere," somewhere between Kever Rachel and Me'aras HaMachpeilah. The driver, an expert on the *mekomos hakedoshim* who often took people on *tiyulim,* was surprised; he didn't know of any holy place in the vicinity. Nevertheless, he was here only to accommodate his passengers, so he pulled over. Soon he and Rav Moshe's children would discover the secret of this very holy place.

Rav Moshe and his children stepped out of the van and stood at the edge of a cliff, where, as far as the eye could see, more mountain ranges extended. Rav Moshe cried out emotionally,

"Look, *ti'ere kinderlach*. From this spot, on the holiest day of the year, Yom Kippur, the *sa'ir laAzazel* (the goat sent to Azazel), was thrown off a cliff, to atone for all the sins of Klal Yisrael. Every year, the Yidden would wait until the goat was sent away, signaling that they had been forgiven for their sins."

The older children were already aware of the purpose of the *sa'ir laAzazel*, but the younger children were fascinated. However, all of them must have wondered why their father was so moved. This was not the Kosel or Kever Rachel. They were just peering out over an empty mountain cliff.

With even more emotion, Rav Moshe continued, "*Kinderlach,* do you remember what you learned in *cheder*? The one who brought the *sa'ir laAzazel* to its destination, the *ish iti*, would not live out the year. You must always remember that even though this person was not going to live out the year, long lines of *chashuve Yidden* clamored to carry out this sacred mission. Why? Because they knew that through them, Klal Yisrael would be cleansed, achieving *kapparah* for their sins."

In a choked voice, Rav Moshe continued, "We must learn a *mussar haskel nora*, an awesome lesson, from this. Look how far a Yid must go — even to be prepared to give up his life — to do a *tovah,* a favor, for another Yid!"

As he gazed over the mountaintop, tears streamed down Rav Moshe's face. He davened and cried to the *Ribbono Shel Olam* to end this bitter exile. "If the *galus* continues because of *sinas chinam*," he prayed, "look, *Aibeshter*, at Your *kinderlach,* and how much we love one another. How much we are willing to sacrifice for another Yid!"

And that is the secret of this holy place, bequeathed to Rav Moshe's children by their father.

GEVURAH

Breaking Rules

We live in a world where technology is moving at the speed of light, or so it seems. Thirty years ago, it was almost unheard of to have a cell phone, and today it is almost unheard of not to.

Everyone recognizes the inherent danger of having unfiltered access to the Internet. Still, depending on one's background and needs, our rabbanim have recommended various forms and methods with which to filter smartphones, or, at times, to minimize their use altogether, and keep us and our families safe from the dangers of secular society.

This story highlights the struggle of one young lady, the guidance she received, and the power one possesses when exhibiting the strength and self-control to take those recommended measures.

The specifics speak to her personal story, but there is a broader message, as well.

RAV CHAIM ZAID WAS ONCE INVITED TO SPEAK AT A Shabbaton for teenage girls, many of whom were struggling. It's not that they were not *shomer Shabbos*; they were. But they felt restricted by many practices, which, they felt, were too confining. This Shabbos was designed to help those girls improve their overall positivity toward Yiddishkeit. After the *seudah* on Friday night, there were many separate workshops. When those were over and it was already late, Rav Zaid addressed all the young women in a plenary session. He delivered a captivating speech and inspired the girls to always grow and become better, to reach beyond themselves, beyond their limitations. One of the suggestions he made was in regard to the use of smartphones.

After Rav Zaid finished speaking, one girl approached him, introduced herself as Batya, and asked to speak to him. Although the hour was very late and he was tired, it was clear she had a pressing issue on her mind, so he agreed.

"I just spent 4,000 shekel on an unfiltered smartphone, but I don't use it for anything wrong. Is that a problem?"

"It's like walking in the street holding a very dangerous instrument," Rav Zaid explained. "Merely holding onto such an instrument can endanger someone's life. Since your phone has the potential to cause immense damage, you should not keep it." He felt that if she was asking him, he could tell it to her straight.

Yet though Batya seemed to be processing his words, she was afraid to take the next step. "It's very difficult for me. Do you know how hard I worked for that 4,000 shekel? I put away a little bit every month and I saved up slowly. Now you're asking me to get rid of it?" But then she thought some more and stated, "Fine, I will do it on one condition."

Rav Zaid listened carefully. "I have a little sister who is only eighteen months old. A short while ago, she came down with a dangerous virus that affected her breathing. The doctors say that her lungs are not working properly and there's nothing to do about it. It's only a matter of time. In the meantime, my mother sits at her bedside day and night. She won't leave her for a minute."

Rav Zaid thought he saw where this was heading and began structuring a response in his mind, but then Batya continued, and what she said wasn't at all what he had expected. "I'll tell you what. I'm prepared to throw away my phone on the condition that the rav will give me a blessing that my sister should die."

Rav Zaid was taken by surprise. What a request! He had never heard such a thing before.

"I'm sorry. I refuse to daven that a *bas Yisrael* should die. *Chas ve'shalom*! Instead, I am going to daven that she should get better."

Batya pleaded, "*Kvod harav*, there is no hope for her. The doctors already determined that there's no way she can live with her lung ailment. Please save my mother and our whole family the pain and agony of watching her suffer!"

Rav Zaid felt Batya's *tzaar*, though he could not begin to imagine the pain of a mother sitting at her child's bedside knowing there was nothing to do but wait. Nonetheless, he persisted. "It may be true that she has no hope through natural means, but you have to know that someone who breaks his *yetzer*, especially with an overwhelming struggle like yours, can merit miracles. We eat round matzos on the night of the Seder, to symbolize the world, which is round, and its natural order. However, when we come to *Yachatz,* we break the round matzos, symbolizing that when we break the *teva*, the rules of our own nature and our natural inclinations, that gives us the ability to effect *nissim,* miracles!"

They continued to speak for another hour. Rav Zaid gently prodded Batya until she promised to throw away her phone. As if to finalize the deal, the two of them recited two *perakim* of *Tehillim* for Batya's baby sister.

In the middle of the week, Rav Zaid received a phone call. Somehow — miraculously, of course — Batya's sister had begun to breathe on her own. After processing this amazing news, Rav Zaid asked when the turnaround had transpired, and was told it was at the time that he and Batya had finalized their phone deal and recited two chapters of *Tehillim*. Over the next week, there was more improvement, and the next week even more. The doctors did not understand what was happening. They said that through natural means this was an impossibility; they couldn't understand why she was still alive, let alone thriving.

When the little girl's recovery was complete, Rav Zaid was

invited to a *seudas hodaah,* where he spoke and revealed that the *yeshuah* had begun precisely when Batya had brought a 4,000-shekel sacrifice.

We have no mizbei'ach today upon which to sacrifice our korbanos, but we can dedicate ourselves fully to Hashem. And when we do, each act of mesirus nefesh has the power to turn the world on its head.

Miracles can — and will — happen.

A Stitch of Sanctity

Rav Nosson Gestetner, a brilliant talmid chacham, wrote tens of sefarim and kuntrussen. In his sefer She'eiris Nosson, he tells a story that reveals the holiness found in even pashute Yidden.

The Nazis destroyed almost the entire cemetery in Lublin; few graves remain, though we can still find the graves of some well-known gedolim, including the Maharshal (Rav Shlomo Luria), Rav Shalom Shachna, and the Chozeh of Lublin (Rav Yaakov Yitzchak Horowitz).

Rav Nosson shared that at one point, the cemetery contained a kever of a lesser-known tzaddik, whose matzeivah read: "Here lies a bachur, a tailor, who triumphed over his yetzer, more than Yosef HaTzaddik."

Although the story is hundreds of years old, it should resonate with today's teenagers, growing up in a challenging society. With lures and temptations unlike any seen in our history, our teenagers must know the value of their struggle against the yetzer hara, and how valued it is in the eyes of the Al-mighty.

YOEL, THE TAILOR'S APPRENTICE, WORKED HARD AT HIS trade, earning himself an excellent reputation. Before long, his name reached the ears of the local *poritz*, the cruel non-Jewish landowner who owned the majority of the land and the homes in the region, and wielded vast power. Upon hearing of the young man's expertise, he grew eager to benefit from his talent and invited Yoel to his palatial home, promising to pay handsomely.

Yoel knew he had no choice in the matter. He understood he was better off appearing voluntarily than being forced to come before the *poritz,* and so he went. As soon as Yoel arrived, the *poritz* welcomed the unsuspecting young man into his home and gave him a large order to fill, offering him a place in the palace where he could work in a comfortable setting. With a spacious workshop and all the fabric he could ever hope for at his disposal, Yoel worked diligently, producing one fine-looking garment after another.

One day, the *poritz* entered his workshop and engaged Yoel in conversation. Yoel had no interest in speaking, but the *poritz* would not be put off. "Tell me, what do you think about as you sew the clothing for my wife and daughter?"

The boy would not give an inch, adamantly refusing to discuss anything in connection with the womenfolk of the *poritz's* home. "I think about not cutting the dress too long or too short." Nothing else.

Though he understood what he was up against, the *poritz* wasn't about to let his Jewish tailor off the hook. Each day, he came in, attempting to wear Yoel down. But the boy proved strong and resilient. His answer was always the same: He focused only on his work, nothing more.

One day, the *poritz's* daughter inquired about the talented young tailor. Though Yoel was clearly not in the same social class as the landowner and his family, the *poritz* was eager to make his pampered daughter happy and presented his request — read: demand — to Yoel.

"I want you to convert and marry my daughter."

Yoel was horrified. *Chas ve'shalom*! What could possibly be worse?

He didn't want to acknowledge the request and hoped it didn't warrant a response, but the *poritz* quickly repeated his statement, and the tailor had to make it clear he would hear nothing of it. He may not have been the most learned young man; he merely sewed clothes. But his beliefs were strong and he fiercely opposed the notion of even entering into a discussion about it.

Now the *poritz* turned angry. Neither he nor his daughter were used to receiving no for an answer. He repeated his demand, this time with the amendment that Yoel did not even have to convert. Marriage would suffice.

Yoel responded with a confident "No!"

Until now, the *poritz* had been fairly certain he could sway the young tailor, but now he realized Yoel was a formidable opponent. He stood face to face with the Jewish man, clearly no longer just a boy, and warned him, "Either marry my daughter — or else."

When Yoel refused, the *poritz* lost patience and ordered him beaten, and his henchmen gladly carried out his wishes.

Over and over, the *poritz* asked.

Over and over, Yoel refused.

The refusal grew in its boldness, and with each refusal more blows rained down on the *bachur*.

Soon, the *poritz* joined in the beatings. Harder and harder. With more fury and more venom.

Until, in a fit of rage and with one final torrent of blows, the *poritz* took the young *tzaddik*'s life.

Feeling defeated, the *poritz* walked away, instructing his henchmen to dump Yoel's body on the road, with a detailed warning to the Jewish community that this is what happens when one refuses to marry the daughter of the *poritz*. The *chevrah kaddisha* retrieved the holy body and the following day, his grieving but very proud family buried their child.

Another Yosef HaTzaddik.

His *matzeivah* bears witness to his defiance, piety, and strength.

Hundreds of years ago, a young man, completely on his own, exhibited "Yosefesque gevurah," and today we continue to draw strength from that tzidkus and kedushah.

Note: When I went to the beis hachaim in Lublin, I didn't see this kever. Perhaps it was destroyed along with the many other kevarim in the cemetery. But through his story, the holy "pashute" tzaddik's struggle and gevurah live on, still inspiring and strengthening others.

His Father

Soon after a boy enters eighth grade, he usually begins to come into his own. It is a short while after his bar mitzvah, which generally triggers his induction into manhood. Along with that come opportunities to speak in public.

For the last 25 years, I've been privileged to teach eighth-graders. About 15 years ago, as part of their initiation into adult life, I began a nice practice. Every Friday, each boy gives a speech to the class, a two-minute dvar Torah or story on a topic I give them, with a fictitious but often plausible scenario as the backdrop. Some of the settings are common occurrences and some a little more far-fetched. For instance, sometimes they act as if they're speaking at a brother's birthday bash or a goodbye party. On other occasions, it's their cousin's bar mitzvah, sister's sheva berachos, nephew's pidyon haben, or other common get-togethers that frequent the cycle of Jewish life. I've also asked them to speak at various communal gatherings, such as the opening of a hachnasas orchim house, a suit store's grand opening (where The Hat Box generously sponsors a shirt, tie, and cuff links for the winner), and I've even asked them to speak at halftime of the Super Bowl!

The winner of the speech, voted in by his peers in a blind vote, wins a pizza lunch. Moreover, the program builds the boys' self-esteem and confidence, and they often become really good at public speaking along the way.

IN 2021, ON THE FRIDAY OF *PARASHAS LECH LECHA*, I GAVE the boys the assignment of speaking at a relative's *bris*. One by one, the boys got up and presented beautiful two-minute speeches on the topic of *bris milah*. Some shared stories of *mesirus nefesh* in times of war and other extenuating circumstances, while others offered insightful *divrei Torah*. Finally, it was Elchonon's turn. I had taught Elchonon's three brothers and they all spoke well; I looked forward to hearing from him, too.

In his two minutes, Elchonon delivered one of the most thought-provoking and mesmerizing speeches I've ever heard — from anyone, at any age. This is what he said:

"It is an honor to address you at my nephew's *bris*. It is so wonderful to be here together with family and friends, in this lovely hall, decorated so nicely for the *simchah*. But I'd like to tell you about another *bris*, which took place at a different time and under a different set of circumstances. The *bris* I'd like to speak about took place 35 years ago. It was my father's *bris*."

As Elchonon spoke, I quickly made a calculation in my mind.

I had taught an older brother who was currently about 25 years old, so how could his father have had his *bris* only 35 years ago? Something was off. But Elchonon was still speaking, so I tuned back in. "His *bris* could not take place when he was 8 days old. Because in the Soviet Union, it was forbidden to have a *bris* and do many other mitzvos. So when my father was 24 years old (!), he met a *mohel* in a tunnel underground, and that's where his *bris* took place."

At this point, I could not believe what I was hearing. I knew that Elchonon's father was from the Former Soviet Union, but who could have imagined such *mesirus nefesh*? Of course, Elchonon now had the class's undivided attention, and they listened to the rest of his speech with bated breath.

"Even my father's parents, uncles, siblings, and cousins didn't know his plans. There was no food and there were no decorations. It was nothing like a *bris* we have nowadays. My father could have been thrown into jail, or worse, for what he did. He risked his life for his *bris milah*. In some ways, my father was like Avraham Avinu, who also underwent a *bris* later in life."

With that, Elchonon sat down.

With tears in my eyes, I thanked Elchonon for his magnificent speech and told the class that I think something very special had just taken place. Everyone clapped and made Elchonon feel good about himself.

It was great. No, it was more than great; it was epic. And to think that I had no idea whatsoever that his father had displayed such heroism and courage.

As soon as Elchonon completed his speech, the *menahel,* Rabbi Yaakov Schwartz, walked into the room. He often comes by for the speeches, as they provide him with an opportunity to compliment the *talmidim*. Even though Elchonon had just finished, I asked him to stand up again and repeat his speech. Surprised at how passionate I was about his story, Elchonon stood up a bit reluctantly and said it again.

Rabbi Schwartz's reaction was no different from mine. If anything, it was more pronounced. He asked Elchonon, "Do you understand that that's why you're here? It's only because of such sacrifice that you are here today. Do you realize that?"

"No!" I corrected, "That's why we're *all* here!"

Elchonon nodded and smiled as he made his way back to his seat for the second time.

Maybe he realizes it, and maybe he is just too young right now. Perhaps he was just happy that a few minutes later, his peers voted him unanimously as the winner of the speech. But one day, he will recognize the eternal bond the Jewish people have with our Creator and what his father gave up to cement that bond. And when it hits him, he will be even more awed than we were.

After all, it's his father.

The Shots Never Fired

Throughout our history, many have threatened the purity and truth of Torah life. Unfortunately, they've frequently come from our own ranks, beginning in the time of the Beis HaMikdash. Starting in the 1700s, it was the Haskalah movement that wreaked havoc in Jewish homes, as its members exhorted the youth to get their heads out of the sand and see the beauty of the "real world." Many young Jews succumbed to their tantalizing offers of freedom and emancipation, and thousands of Jewish children were lost. The movement continued in full strength through the next century.

In the early 1900s, though Haskalah's influence had died down, there were still others who wanted to "enlighten" their Jewish brothers and water down their observance and their children's education, and the gedolim continued to fight and urge communities to ignore the enticing but empty promises.

The following story, told by Rav Don Segal, illustrates the courage and conviction of one such Torah leader.

RAV AVRAHAM KALMANOWITZ FIRST SERVED AS THE RAV of Rakov (in Belarus) and later as rosh yeshivah of Yeshivas Mir in Brooklyn, New York, where he built Torah from the ground up. During World War II, he worked tirelessly to save as many Jews as he could from the Nazi inferno. This was aside from the many Sephardic and Russian Jews he rescued later on. Even while still in Europe, he saved many Jews from their spiritual enemies.

Between the two World Wars, Rav Avraham traveled to Belgium to collect money to help the yeshivos in Eastern Europe, which were struggling to survive. While there, he received an emergency telegram from his hometown of Rakov, stating that "enlightened" Jews were threatening to take over the town.

As it was, the irreligious Jews had developed a stronghold in the region and infiltrated the minds of young adults, who were now gathering to share ideas and various plans of action. And now they were planning on building a school to teach "culture." That would be the final nail in the coffin. The senders of the telegrams begged Rav Avraham to return immediately; the situation had turned dire.

Rav Avraham abandoned everything and traveled back home. He knew what was at stake. His first course of action was to ask all the *baalei batim* to refuse to rent any space to the organizers of the school; that would at least stall all operations. Yet merely trying to prevent these "cultured" Jews from opening a school would not be enough. Eventually, they would find another starting point. He felt the need to do more.

The rav announced that he would be speaking at a large gathering on the upcoming Friday night after the Shabbos *seudah*, in the main shul of Rakov. When the members of the other camp got wind of Rav Avraham's intentions, they sent a vicious warning, stating that if he followed through, they would kill him on the spot!

Rav Avraham's family members pleaded with him not to go. These wicked people didn't mess around. Tragically, Dr. Jacob Israël de Haan, the political spokesman of *chareidi* Jewry in Yerushalayim in the 1920s, had recently been murdered by a bunch of anti-religious Jewish ruffians. Rav Avraham's adversaries wouldn't hesitate to do the same to him.

But Rav Avraham would not be deterred. He fearlessly moved forward, unfazed by the threats. On Friday afternoon, he brought his *ksav rabbanus* with him to shul. After the *seudah*, with the shul filled to capacity, he walked to the front, scanned the room, and addressed the entire town, including the leaders of the opposition, with passion and power.

"It used to be that the rav of the city was the only voice regarding all important matters. Now, these 'free-thinking' Jews have tried to take it all away. Even so, one thing remains under the guidance of the rav, and that's the *chinuch* of the town. Yet these people are trying to take that, as well. They are trying to rip away the future of our children. Know this. If they succeed in what they are trying to do, then I am returning my letter of appointment as rav of this city. You will have no further need for me."

With the eyes of the entire city watching his every move, the rav turned around to the *aron kodesh*, pushed aside the *paroches*, and cried out, "*Ribbono Shel Olam*, so-called 'enlightened' Jews have warned me that if I try to stop them and oppose their efforts, they will kill me. But I am standing up for Your honor. And I will not be intimidated." He then stepped down, walked up to his antagonists, and gave them a piece of his mind, chastising them for their efforts and reiterating that he would not be intimidated.

The shul was silent as the rav opened up his long coat and with an air of defiance, dared his opponents, "Shoot me!"

Not a soul moved. With fire in his eyes, the Rav Avraham stood there and stared them down.

Finally, he walked away, exited the shul, and headed back to his home in peace.

Word of the incident reached the Chofetz Chaim, who expressed his admiration for Rav Avraham and praised his courage, recounting the story and concluding, "The Rakover Rav taught us what it means to be a rav."

Today, there is nothing left of the "isms" and movements of that generation. But there are other forces of anti-Torah leadership threatening the authenticity and purity of our holy Torah and our sacred way of life. We must be inspired by Rav Kalmanowitz and others like him, who stood up for the honor of Hashem.

The battle continues.

But: "Moshe emes ve'Soraso emes."

The unmitigated truth of Torah will always prevail.

Sticks and Stones May Break My Bones

We all know how careful we must be with our speech. But how far are we willing to go not to speak badly about another Jew? Rav Yaakov Galinsky endured horrible suffering to do so.

AS A YOUNG MAN, YANKELE WAS EXILED TO SIBERIA. Despite the bitter cold, he was given only skimpy garb, not enough to provide even a modicum of warmth. Additionally, the portions of food were paltry, further exacerbating Yankele's suffering. However, although he was physically compromised, his strength of spirit ignited his soul and warmed his heart.

One day, while he was walking in the labor camp, another Jew stopped him and offered a deal he could not refuse. Though Yankele had some cash, he could not simply buy food with it. Only special coupons could purchase food, and those were worth more than gold. Now this Jew was offering Yankele an extra coupon with which to obtain rations. Happy to secure additional nourishment, Yankele gladly handed over the sum he requested. He had no reason to suspect that the coupon had been stolen from the commander's room — which it was.

Glad to satiate his gnawing hunger, Yankele stood in line, eagerly waiting his turn. At the moment that he waited in line, however, the commander noticed that a coupon had been stolen from his room. Infuriated, he resolved to find the perpetrator and give him the beating of his life. He instructed the officer in charge of food distribution that when he comes across the coupon — and he told the officer how he'd be able to identify it — the officer should grab the prisoner and bring him straight to the commander's office.

Finally, Yankele's turn came and he asked for some bread and drink. As soon as he placed the coupon into the officer's hand, though, the officer grabbed him and forcibly brought him to the commander, who demanded to know why Yankele had stolen the coupon from his room. Yankele pleaded innocent, claiming he knew nothing about the coupon's origins. "I didn't steal anything. I just bought a coupon for full price."

Yankele's alleged lie and calm demeanor only incensed the commander even more. "Tell me immediately who sold you the coupon. If not, you're going to regret it, I promise you."

Knowing full well what the consequences could be, Yankele made up his mind not to say a word. "I'm not going to tell you who sold me the coupon. I refuse to tattle on another Jew."

By now, the commander was fit to be tied. In a frenzy of anger, he hollered, "If you don't tell me immediately who sold you the coupon, I'm going to take your fingers and stick them between the door and the frame. And then we'll see how well you can hold your tongue."

Yankele would not be intimidated; the commander had no idea whom he was dealing with. Not only did Yankele refuse to talk, but he chose to admonish the commander. "Among Jews, snitching is a grievous sin. It's much worse than having your hand crushed."

That was it. The seething commander grabbed Yankele's hand and placed his fingers around the doorframe and with all of his might, slammed the door, shattering them. It would take many long months for his hand to heal, and for the rest of his life, he suffered because of those breaks. But there was more to come.

The commander had placed the fear of heaven in each of the inmates. Absolutely everyone was terrified of him.

Everyone, that is, except for the 20-year-old defiant Jew.

It bothered him to no end that Yankele disobeyed his command, making a mockery of him, the high commander. His sense of defeat caused him to lose his ability to think rationally, and he warned Yankele, "Everyone here bows before me. You are the only one who refused. I want you to know that I can take revenge on you at any moment. And I will!"

Uncertain what to do next, he grabbed a small bottle of ink from his table and threw it at Yankele. Yankele dodged it at the last moment, and the bottle hit the wall, smashing into glass splinters everywhere, and causing a big black blotch on the wall. All this only served to escalate the commander's fury. He grabbed Yankele, threw him to the floor, and began beating him, all while screaming and yelling and demanding that he reveal the name of the coupon thief. By now, Yankele felt like he was on the verge of death, but he still refused to divulge the Jew's name. Struggling to breathe, he whispered a prayer that he be granted the strength to keep his secret.

His prayer was answered. A few minutes later, the disgruntled commander stormed out of the office, leaving Yankele writhing in pain, barely able to move, but free to leave. Eventually, bruised and bloodied, Yankele mustered the strength to stand on his feet and make his way out of the office.

As he hobbled back to his barracks, a small smile formed on his face.

His secret was safe.

And so was the Jew whose life he had spared.

Truth Be Told

The following story, shared by Rav Yitzchak Shkop in his sefer MeIsh LeRei'eihu, speaks of sacrifice, courage, and kindness. Most of all, it speaks of truth. At all costs.

RAV MANNIS ZITNITZKY LOST HIS WIFE AND SIX CHILdren in the Holocaust. After the war, he remarried, but he and his wife were not *zocheh* to build a new family. They lived in the Neve Achiezer neighborhood in Bnei Brak, a neighborhood of Holocaust survivors like them, who epitomized *emunah* and *bitachon.* A prominent Gerrer Chassid, Rav Mannis established Yeshivas Imrei Emes.

Every Friday, Rav Yisrael Zev Shkop, who lived near Rav Mannis's neighborhood in Bnei Brak, sent his son Yitzchak to Rav Mannis for a *bechinah* on the *parashah* and a warm piece of potato kugel. Generally, young children don't enjoy spending time with older people, unless they are their grandparents. At times, Yitzchak wanted to play with his friends on Fridays and not go to Rav Mannis, and wondered why he, and not his friends, had to go. His father, wanting to mitigate some of Rav Mannis's pain due to childlessness, insisted he go. But it was only years after Rav Mannis's passing that Rav Yisrael Zev told his son a story that fully solved the mystery.

In middle of World War II, the Germans set up a factory in the Lodz ghetto to produce boots for their soldiers. With the war moving ahead at full throttle, the foot soldiers were fighting with the Russian soldiers in frozen conditions. The fighter pilots, as well, complained of the frigid weather and its dangers. If the soldiers had any chance to survive long enough to win the war, they would need warm, fur-lined boots, and quickly. To that end, the Germans offered food rations and preferential treatment to the factory's workers.

However, since the Nazis could not afford any mess-ups, only expert shoemakers were accepted. They warned that if they discovered employees lying about their credentials, they would be put to death on the spot. Knowing the Nazis, this was no empty threat.

The Germans appropriated a warehouse and placed various groups in different parts of the building. Some were in a larger room, and some in smaller sections. Each group in the factory was comprised of ten individuals, and was responsible for the formation and the construction of the boots from the beginning of the process until the end.

Yisrael Zev Shkop was less than an expert when it came to shoemaking, but knew that entry into such a group was a ticket to life. Determined to try his luck, he approached the foreman of one such group and requested to join. When asked if he knew anything about shoemaking, he admitted he knew nothing. The foreman barked at him and told him to disappear immediately.

Disappointed, Yisrael Zev approached other groups, four or five of them, but the response was always the same. Afraid for their own lives, no one wanted anything to do with him.

Seeing his chances dwindling and time ticking away, Yisrael Zev resolved to ask two more groups and then, if he had no choice, he would have to bend the truth. He walked up to the next group and repeated his routine, this time with a little more desperation in his voice. For the first time, the foreman seemed a bit sympathetic, looking at him a little longer than the others had. However, when the foreman asked the defining question — "Do you have experience with shoes?" — Yisrael Zev told the absolute truth that no, he knew nothing of the trade. This time, instead of sending him away, the man told him, "Listen, *bachur*, here is a bucket of black dye. We need someone to mix it continuously so it doesn't congeal. Sit down here, stick your hands in, and keep stirring."

Incredibly grateful for the chance to extend his life, Yisrael Zev got to work. He stuck his right hand into the bucket and moved it around vigorously. When the foreman came back to check on him and saw that his left hand was clean, he told Yisrael Zev to stick both hands in to make sure all of the dye could be put to use. A few minutes later, he returned. Noting that both of Yisrael Zev's hands were black, he exclaimed, "Congratulations! You're a shoemaker!"

And just in the nick of time.

Right then, a Nazi soldier burst through the door and marched around, searching for a fraud. He claimed there was an imposter who claimed to be proficient in shoemaking when he wasn't even a novice. Yisrael Zev sensed he was just a moment away from death. But then the foreman spoke up. "The young man you are looking for is right here, in my group, based upon my request. Now, please take a look at his hands. He's an excellent shoemaker." The German guard gave a quick inspection and sized up Yisrael Zev. Convinced he was legitimate, he turned around and left just as quickly as he had come.

After sharing this story with Yitzchak, Rav Yisrael Zev delivered the punchline. "Do you know who that foreman was? None other than Rav Mannis Zitnitzky. It is he to whom I owe my life!" Now Yitzchak understood why Rav Mannis often referred to him as his *einekel*.

But Yitzchak had one more question. "Why didn't you tell the first foreman you were a shoemaker? Why did you plan on waiting until you were at the end of your rope?"

Rav Yisrael Zev's answer, though simple, spoke volumes about his character, integrity, *gevurah,* and overall makeup.

"Because I'm not a shoemaker."

The Easy Road

The following story of suspense and intrigue is fascinating on its own, but the lesson it carries is perhaps more valuable.

AN ELDERLY MAN, MR. MICHEL WEISSWASSER, WHO HAD no family of his own, lived near the dormitory of an Israeli yeshivah and enjoyed spending time with the *bachurim*. The boys loved the friendly, sweet man, and took care of him; if he needed food or medicine or an errand, the *bachurim* were all too happy to help him out.

When Mr. Weisswasser fell ill, the *bachurim* took turns visiting him in the hospital. A short time later, he was pronounced healthy enough to return home and the boys breathed a sigh of relief for their elderly friend. But a few days later, when he didn't show up for davening in the morning, the *bachurim* knew something was wrong. They ran to his apartment and found him lifeless.

Although they were very sad at the loss of their friend, there was no time to sit and cry. They had to act quickly, for time was of the essence. Our story takes place in the middle of the 20th century, when the Israeli government sanctioned (or at best did nothing to prevent) the performance of autopsies, especially when there was no family member to object. The *bachurim* knew Mr. Weisswasser's *guf* was a perfect candidate for desecration, so they hatched a plan.

By the time the police arrived, Mr. Weisswasser's body was no longer in his home; the boys had brought him to the dormitory. Somehow, the police officers found out where Mr. Weisswasser had been taken, but when they came to the dorm, the door was locked. Though they banged and banged, no one answered. Finally, they began to force their way in. After a few minutes, they managed to make their way into the building and were appalled by what they saw. The entire stairwell, from the ground floor all the way up to the third floor, was filled with beds and bed frames. Not only that, but the boys had poured water and oil all over the steps, to make it even more difficult for the policemen to climb the stairs.

The police officers understood that this was more than just a prank. This was a fight for the dignity of an old man, the fight for the sanctity of the Jewish body.

Nevertheless, they had been given their instructions by the higher-ups, so they proceeded. They certainly had their work cut out for them. It took them six hours to move all the mattresses and beds, bed by bed and frame by frame. The steps were indeed slippery and the policemen had to be extremely careful. At long last, they reached the third floor and found a body on a stretcher, covered with a *tallis*. The officers carried it down the steps, placed it inside the ambulance, turned on the lights and the sirens, and sped off to the Institute of Abu Kabir, where an autopsy was scheduled.

About 15 minutes later, they received the shock of their lives.

First the body began to move, and then it sat up!

The *tallis* fell away, and there sat a *bachur,* very much alive.

The entire distraction had been created to confuse the authorities and make them think Mr. Weisswasser's body was on the third floor. In truth, it was on ground level. Without saying a word, they had led the police to assume that since the barricades were on the stairwell, the body was on the third floor.

Although the police officers were extremely frustrated, there was nothing to do. By the time they discovered the plot, the old man was buried, his dignity preserved.

Rav Yisrael Altman shared this story and gleaned from it a very powerful lesson. Sometimes, the yetzer hara will "stack the stairwell" to prevent us from accomplishing our goals. He will do his utmost to stop us from learning or performing noble acts and deeds.

At other times, he is even smarter. Instead of scheming to block us from achieving our goals, he leaves the path to success wide open. However, we never give the easy road any merit or validity, but assume there is nothing of value to be found on the unobstructed path.

This, Rav Altman says, occurs when we fail to take advantage of something reachable and easy to do, such as davening. The shuls and minyanim are accessible, minyanim readily available. All types of siddurim with translation and inspiration lie at our fingertips.

There are so many other examples of easy mitzvos, there for the taking. Whenever we meet someone, we can greet them with a friendly smile and hello, but do we? We can offer rides to others when we are going out anyway. We can help family members so easily; they are right there in the same house as us! The list goes on.

Let's not be fooled when the yetzer hara stacks the stairwell.

Instead, let us grab the opportunity while it's right there, ready for the taking.

EMUNAH

Of Course

EVERY YEAR ON THE 14TH OF IYAR, THE *YAHRTZEIT* OF the holy Tanna, Rabbi Meir Baal HaNess, many Jews travel to his *kever* in Teveriah, where they pour out their hearts in prayer. One year, a group of men and women from Neve Yaakov decided to turn this day into a *yom tefillah,* to daven at the gravesites of other *tzaddikim* in northern Eretz Yisrael, as well. They chartered a bus and it filled quickly.

After traveling about two hours, the bus dropped them off at Rabbi Meir's *kever* and drove off. The men and women split up and spent an hour davening. With all the hubbub and chaos, it wasn't easy to concentrate. Conversely, in a certain way, the sheer volume of Yidden in this holy place added to their experience and influenced their *tefillos*. All in all, it was a good start to the day.

The next stop would be quite different.

As they arrived at Kfar Chakuk, the burial site of Chavakuk HaNavi, the difference was stark. At the *kever* of Rabbi Meir Baal HaNess, hundreds, perhaps even thousands, were coming and going. But in Kfar Chakuk, aside from the passengers on the bus from Neve Yaakov, there was only an elderly custodian, Gideon. Dressed in his little cap and weighed down by his keys, he welcomed them and gave them a box of candles in case they wanted to light a candle, as some do.

Gideon also gave his guests some insight into Chavakuk. The name חבקוק is rooted in the word חיבוק, a hug. In *II Melachim,* we read about the childless *ishah haShunamis,* who took pains to host Elisha HaNavi in an honorable manner and was promised (4:16), "*La'moed hazeh ka'es chayah at chovekes* (חובקת) *ben* — At this season next year you will be hugging a son." Thus, when the prophecy was fulfilled, she named her son Chavakuk. Chavakuk later received another hug from Elisha, when the *navi* brought the lifeless child back to life. This child grew up to be Chavakuk HaNavi, one of the defenders of Klal Yisrael. Hearing the background about the illustrious Chavakuk inspired the crowd to daven with even more *kavanah,* and each one asked for his respective *yeshuah.*

After they finished, a discussion ensued as to where to eat the lunch they had brought with them; it was going to be a long day and they needed strength to daven properly. While some recommended they eat right there — there was a tent set up for such a purpose — the more vocal of the group suggested they first go to the *kever* of Rabbi Shimon bar Yochai, and after davening there, they could enjoy their lunch.

It was only about 30 minutes to Meron, where Rabbi Shimon is buried; they certainly could wait a bit longer to eat. So they boarded the bus and headed out to the *kever* of Rabbi Shimon bar Yochai. As soon as they arrived, though, it began to pour. This was a surprise; they had checked the weather forecast and rain had not been called for. Though it rarely rains in Eretz Yisrael from Pesach until Succos, a torrential, unforgiving storm pummeled Meron. One by one, the passengers got off the bus and ran into the *tziyun* to daven.

Although they were able to daven, there was no way they could eat there. They didn't want to eat inside the *tziyun,* and it didn't look like the rain was going to let up anytime soon. With their hunger growing, they began discussing their options. While there were many, for some reason, the most popular suggestion was to return to the *kever* of Chavakuk and eat in the tent there.

They boarded the bus and made their way back to Kfar Chakuk. No sooner had they entered the village than the rain stopped. Not only that, but it appeared as if it had not rained at all in that area.

Strange.

They quickly began to set up lunch, pans of lamb and *pargiot* (chicken thighs) along with salad, *techina*, and fresh pita. Before they went to wash, the men invited Gideon, the caretaker who had inspired them with words about Chavakuk earlier, to join them. He happily obliged and they quickly made a plate for him and provided him with a seat.

They sang songs and shared *divrei Torah* and, feeling satiated, prepared to *bentch*. But before they did, Gideon asked to say a few words. *Why not*? they thought.

Gideon stood up and spoke in a raspy voice. "When you first arrived at the *kever*, I was not feeling well. I hadn't had a chance to eat breakfast before coming to work, so I was very hungry. I heard you speaking about the possibility of eating lunch here and, assuming you'd invite me to join you, I was very pleased. But then, when you decided to go elsewhere, I was too embarrassed to ask you to give me something. However, now I want to apologize to you..."

Apologize? they wondered. *For what?*

"When you left, I began to daven to Hashem and I told Him I was hungry. So I'm sorry that because of me you *had* to come back..."

And then it hit them. It was not supposed to rain in the region; the rainstorm in Meron had taken them by surprise. But because of the sudden downpour, they'd ended up returning to Kfar Chakuk for lunch.

Of course, they had.

Because a Yid in Kfar Chakuk was hungry and had davened to Hashem, asking Him for food. Gideon said it plainly, as a matter of fact. He knew why this had happened. He was just apologizing to them that he had "forced" them to come back to feed him.

When the group first came to the *kever*, Gideon had also mentioned what Chavakuk is perhaps best known for, for simplifying the entire Torah into one sentence: "*Ve'tzaddik be'emunaso yichyeh* — But the righteous person will live through his faith" (*Chavakuk* 2:4).

And they had just witnessed it firsthand.

The Miracle of Life

Though the suffering of Greek Jewry during World War II is not as well known as that of Jews in other European countries, Greek Jewry endured a greater percentage of loss than almost any other country; nearly 85 percent of the Jews of Salonika (a prominent Greek city, where many Jews resided) were killed, the vast majority in Auschwitz. However, there were those who survived and rebuilt their lives anew.

UPON ARRIVAL AT THE CONCENTRATION CAMP, OVADIAH Baruch, a Greek Jew, was immediately branded with a number on his arm. With no friends or family to turn to, Ovadiah felt his very life seeping out of him. He walked around lethargically, waiting to die. Then, to his immense fortune, he was unexpectedly given the job of doling out soup to his fellow inmates, and his spirits rose. Perhaps there was hope after all. Not only did he have access to food and the kitchen, but he would also be able to help others.

Aliza Tzorfati, also from Greece, was not given preferential treatment. She was sent to the dreaded Block 10, where the cursed Germans conducted medical experiments, often robbing young ladies of their ability to bear children. Aliza walked toward the barracks filled with trepidation and fear, but she soon strengthened her resolve to survive. She would overcome.

As soon as she entered, however, she looked up and saw something that filled her with hatred and disgust. The one performing these experimental procedures was none other than Dr. Samuels, a Jewish doctor! After waiting her turn, she looked at the doctor and asked him one question. "How could you?!" And then with every ounce of anger she could muster, she spit in his face.

It is one thing for a Nazi physician to oversee such medical practices. One would not expect anything more of such ruthless and animalistic creatures. But for a Yid to be performing such procedures? It was unconscionable!

A few moments later, it was over. The procedure would prevent Aliza from ever having children. She was shattered. In truth, she didn't even want to live anymore. For what? For what purpose? If she couldn't rebuild her own family, what point was there in living?

A few days later, she was walking past the men's section of the camp when she heard someone screaming in Greek from behind the barracks. She quickly ran over to see if she could help a Jew from her country, and she noticed a Nazi soldier beating Ovadiah Baruch mercilessly. She didn't know the young man. She only knew that if she didn't do something quickly, the Nazi would end the young man's life. She began to yell and for some reason, the Nazi beast seemed to change his mind and went on his way.

As soon as the guard walked away, Ovadiah, who was reeling from his beating and his wounds, thanked his savior profusely. So overwhelmed was he that he asked Aliza on the spot if she would marry him if they both survived. She laughed at the notion and assured him that he would not want to marry her. He didn't pursue the matter and neither did she. After ensuring that he was all right, she left and went back to the women's camp.

Over the next two years, their paths never crossed. Even so, the story was fresh in Ovadiah's mind. When the camps were liberated, he began to search for Aliza, though he was unable to locate her. Finally, months after they were liberated, he found her.

Although Ovadiah had not seen Aliza in over two years, he could not forget her kindness and asked her to restart her life together with him. Now that the question was for real, she had to reveal why she thought he would not be interested, and recounted the horrendous tale with Dr. Samuels.

However, Ovadiah would not take no for an answer. He was intent on rebuilding with Aliza. If she could not have a family, they would at least have each other and would help others rebuild and begin their lives anew. After much persuasion, Aliza agreed and the two of them got married. A short while later, they picked up and moved to the land of their dreams, Eretz Yisrael.

Then a miracle occurred. A few months later, Aliza was not feeling well and she went to the doctor. The doctor examined her and shared the good news. She was expecting!

She thanked the doctor but insisted it was impossible. When she told him about the nightmare she had experienced, he recommended that she do some research because she was, in fact, expecting a child.

Overjoyed yet extremely curious, she and her husband began to research the matter. They discovered that there were others like her, young women who had encountered Dr. Samuels, but astoundingly were all expecting children. How could it be? And then they investigated further and uncovered Dr. Samuels' secret.

In truth, he had asked to be the one to perform those procedures. Nevertheless, despite strict orders from the Germans under the threat of death, he did not hurt one young Jewish woman. Instead, he saved them all. When the Nazis discovered his charade, they tortured him mercilessly and finally butchered him.

Six months later, Aliza and Ovadiah were holding their beautiful newborn baby boy.

They named him after the *tzaddik*, Dr. Samuels.

There are times in which we experience overwhelming challenges in our lives, and we are certain these events will cause us harm, perhaps permanently. Little do we know that Hashem, the Rofei Chol Basar, has a plan.

Not only would He never hurt His children, but He continuously gives us life, every moment of our existence.

Let Go!

THE ALEXANDER REBBE, RAV YECHIEL DANCYGER, WAS traveling with his son, the Yismach Yisrael, Rav Yerachmiel Yisrael Yitzchak. The Rebbe, an elderly, weak man, suffered from numerous ailments and illnesses. On the trip, he suddenly began to experience the symptoms of a heart attack; he felt faint and lightheaded. Though the Rebbe was in urgent need of medical attention, he and his son were nowhere near a doctor or medical facility. They were on their own.

The Rebbe believed the time had come to say the end-of-life *tefillos*. He held his son's hand and asked him to recite *Viduy* and *Krias Shema* with him. But the Yismach Yisrael reassured him, "Don't worry, Father. Just drink a glass of water and everything will be fine. It's going to be all right. You'll feel better before you know it." He gave his father a glass of water and immediately he began to feel stronger. In fact, he felt much better than he had at the beginning of the trip. His *kochos* were restored.

"Tell me son, how did you know I would begin to feel better, when all indications were that my end was near?"

The Yismach Yisrael responded, "I learned it from David HaMelech."

He explained: In the 13th *kapitel* of *Tehillim* (v. 2), David cries out, "*Ad anah Hashem tishkacheini netzach. Ad anah tastir es panecha mimeni.*" David, who endured much suffering in his lifetime, asks: How long will Hashem act as if He has forgotten him? How long will He hide His face from him?

He wonders how much longer he will have to keep searching for methods and schemes in order to save himself (v. 3): "*Ad anah ashis eitzos be'nafshi.*" In addition, ordinarily a person is happy during the day, but David states that even in the day, his heart is unhappy, for how long will his enemy triumph over him? "*Yagon bilvavi yomam ad anah yarum oyvi alai*" (ibid.).

In the following two verses, he looks up toward Heaven and begs, "*Habitah aneini Hashem Elokai ha'irah einai pen ishan hamaves. Pen yomar oyvi yecholtiv tzarai yagilu ki emot.*" David states, "*Ribbono Shel Olam,* I don't know what to do! This is a matter of life and death. If You don't answer me and enlighten my eyes, I'm going to die, and this may cause my enemy to boast that he overcame me; I don't want my tormentors to rejoice when I stumble."

Almost an entire *perek* is devoted to David HaMelech's despairing *krechtz* of pain.

But then, in the final words of the *perek* (v. 6), David changes course and proclaims, "I am fine since I am putting my faith in You, and soon I will exult in Your salvation; I will sing to You, Hashem, because You were so kind to me: *Va'ani be'chasdecha vatachti yagel libi bi'shuasecha; ashirah laShem ki gamal alai*!"

Why? What changed?

The Yismach Yisrael shared his interpretation. "When a person thinks he is running the show and he's in charge, he believes it's all just a matter of finding the right person to help solve his problems. If he is sick, he will seek the right doctor. If he is in need of a *shidduch,* he will run to the *shadchan*. If he is in need of *parnassah*, he will make his way to an *askan*. In such a case, he needs *zechuyos* to make sure all his plans fall into place.

"However, when a person finds himself in a situation where

he is all alone and there is nobody around, when there is no *shadchan,* no *askan,* no physician in the vicinity, then all he has left is his faith in the Al-mighty. And if one can hold onto his faith, then, '*yagel libi bi'shuasecha; ashirah laShem ki gamal alai.*' His salvation is certain to come and his heart will exult in it, and soon enough he will be singing to Hashem and thanking Him for His kindness."

The Yismach Yisrael addressed his father. "Father, had you fallen ill in Warsaw, where there are thousands of your Chassidim and also excellent doctors, our *bitachon* would have been somewhat compromised. We may have depended on your Chassidim or the physicians, and that's actually reason for concern. But now that this mishap occurred on the road, with no one else around, we had nowhere to turn other than to the Al-mighty, and I wasn't worried at all. For if we are in a state of '*Va'ani be'chasdecha vatachti,*' when we truly trust in the kindness of Hashem, we are *zocheh* to the end of the verse, '*yagel libi bi'shuasecha,*' and our hearts exult in His salvation."

***

An elderly Yerushalmi Yid was standing at the bus stop on Rechov Bar Ilan waiting for the bus to Ramot. Unexpectedly, a car with a *yungerman* and his wife inside stopped right near him.

"Can we offer you a ride to Ramot?"

At first, the Yerushalmi refused. It wasn't nice to intrude on a married couple's private time. Additionally, the woman was sitting in the front seat, and he assumed she would move to the back when he came in; he didn't want to inconvenience her. However, the couple had made the offer, and now they insisted he join them, so he got into the car.

Thankful that he wouldn't have to sit on the bus for the long ride, the Yid felt indebted to his benefactors. He decided to tell them the story of the Alexander Rebbe as a show of his gratitude, and they seemed to appreciate it. When they arrived at his home, he thanked them again and said goodbye.

A half-year later, the Yid was traveling on the bus when the *yungerman* who had offered him a ride approached him. "*Shalom aleichem*. I've been looking for you for such a long time. Do you remember that my wife and I gave you a ride about six months ago?" At first, the Yid didn't remember but when the *yungerman* mentioned the story of the Alexander Rebbe the Yid had recounted, it jogged his memory.

Now the *yungerman* had his own story to tell:

> *My wife and I had been married for years and we had not yet merited children. We went through many procedures and paid a lot of money. Our hopes were dashed numerous times and our spirits crushed. On the day we offered you a ride, we were on our way back from yet another unsuccessful procedure, and we didn't know how much more we could take; it seemed like our world was coming to an end.*
>
> *Though we don't own a car, that day we were driving my father-in-law's car. When we passed the bus stop, we decided to pull up and offer someone a ride to his destination. We hoped that if we showed even a small amount of compassion to someone else, perhaps in that zechus Hashem would bestow His mercy upon us. After all, Chazal say, "Kol hamerachem al habriyos merachamin alav min haShamayim — Anyone who has compassion on Hashem's creatures will receive compassion from Heaven" (Shabbos 151b).*
>
> *At first, you refused the ride we offered and I understood why. But when I persisted, you agreed and "paid us" for our trouble by telling us the story of the Alexander Rebbe and his son.*
>
> *My wife and I saw the story as a Heavenly message. We realized we had become too busy looking for all types of help and had put all of our faith in our doctors and their procedures. Of course, we had to do our hishtadlus, but ultimately, "Va'ani be'chasdecha vatachti yagel libi bi'shuasecha." If we*

place our trust in Hashem's kindness, our hearts will eventually rejoice in His salvation. After hearing your story, we resolved to strengthen ourselves in bitachon and emunah.

A few weeks later, we received the news. My wife is expecting.

"Yagel libi bi'shuasecha!"

After concluding his story, the *yungerman* turned to the Yerushalmi Yid. "I wanted to thank you for the *chizuk*. It changed our lives."

We want so many things to happen, and Hashem wants to give us everything we need. Perhaps if we let go a little more, we will see how tightly He is holding onto us.

The Hows and Whys

Rav Amram Blau, the fearless tzaddik, told a story demonstrating the trust and belief of the Yidden of yesteryear, and what such strong faith can accomplish.

AVREMEL AND MINNA GOTTLIEB LIVED IN EUROPE BEFORE World War II. As they advanced in years, they decided to act upon their lifelong aspiration of moving to Eretz Yisrael. First, though, they had to purchase tickets — but they had no money in the bank. In the prewar years, it was very difficult to make it financially in Europe, and Avremel and Minna were no different from most others. Even after selling all of their belongings, most of which were not worth much, they were still short.

Not so quick to give up on their dream, the Gottliebs decided to go to the port and try their luck there. Arriving with just the barest essentials in their hands, they approached the captain of the first ship they saw and asked if they could purchase tickets. The captain named the price, and when he saw the Gottliebs did not have enough money to fully cover the cost, he apologized but told them no; the sum they were offering would not even allow them to travel in steerage. They tried to board another ship, where the same dialogue ensued.

While Minna was beginning to think it was just not meant to be, Avremel was still holding out and hoping to make it to Eretz Yisrael. He suggested they try to gain passage on a cargo ship, where tickets would be significantly less costly. Leaving Minna behind for a moment, Avremel made his way over to the captain of the cargo ship and asked for a price. The captain quoted a fee they could actually afford, and Avremel began to reach into his satchel to retrieve the money, when the captain added one small caveat. The charge included only ship fare and nothing else. No food. With no other options, Avremel accepted the terms and paid without consulting his wife. He merely let her know he had procured the tickets, and the two of them boarded the ship.

Soon after the ship set sail, Minna mentioned she was hungry and asked Avremel if he had any food. He did not. They'd needed every last penny for the purchase of the tickets, so he'd been unable to buy any provisions for their journey. Minna then assumed the ship would provide meals. Had they been traveling on an ordinary passenger ship, that would have been the case. However, they were passengers on a cargo ship, and the captain had made it clear that the terms did not include food.

When she finally realized what was going on, Minna looked at Avremel incredulously. "You didn't buy provisions and you didn't arrange for meals? What are we going to eat? How are we going to survive on the ship?"

As someone who possessed great *bitachon*, Avremel responded as he always did, "Hashem will provide."

Minna was quick to protest. "It's one thing to live with such an attitude on dry land, where there are many ways to obtain food. But how will we get food here, in the middle of the sea?"

Though Avremel understood her frustration, he wanted to clarify one point. "I know you're concerned. Nevertheless, I want you to be aware that for Hashem, there is no difference between providing food when we're on the ground or when we're at sea. Either way, He can — and He will — provide."

A few weeks later, Avremel and Minna Gottlieb reached the port of Haifa, alive and well.

You may be wondering how they got hold of food. In truth, those particulars take away from the point of the story. Recently, especially with the tragedies the Jewish world has endured, many are often busy with the details. They want to know where, when, and how many. Yet all of that detracts from the message. We think that if we know exactly what happened, we can figure it out; we can see the pattern and understand the plan. And most problematic of all, we think the calamity could have been prevented.

Hashem controls the world.
We must believe and have faith.
Leave the how and why to Him.

***

This reminded me of another piercing story I recounted years ago.

Eli and Shirah had been married seven years. Though it was their most fervent wish, they had not yet been blessed with a child. The treatments they had undergone, the tests, everything had been so trying and so expensive — and all for nothing. They felt their hope slipping away, yet they so badly wanted a baby!

Several *chesed* and support groups helped them through their ordeal. One of those organizations was ATIME, which is devoted to assisting childless Jewish couples yearning for a baby of their own. Eli and Shirah were fortunate to receive the assistance of a very special individual, Rabbi Aron Shmuel Jacobowitz, director of medical affairs of ATIME during that period. Although not a physician, Rabbi Jacobowitz earned the respect of the medical world in helping childless couples. A chassidishe Yid from Williamsburg, he seemed an unlikely individual to be involved in such matters. Nonetheless, his heart was devoted to helping those in need, and he did so much research and read so much on the subject that he earned honorary degrees in this field from some of the most prestigious universities. Reb Aron Shmuel served as the liaison between the hospital or clinic and Eli and Shirah, explaining all of the medical terms and helping them understand what was going on.

Eli and Shirah embraced their challenge with unusual *bitachon* and strength. Yet with each passing day, their burning desire to have a child grew stronger and stronger. Their hearts ached when they saw children playing outside. Each Shabbos and Yom Tov, they'd look at one another, pain and suffering in their eyes, and weep for the children they did not have to sit at their table, laughing and singing. Watching their nieces and nephews say the *Mah Nishtanah*, or seeing them dressed up in their adorable Purim costumes, was so painful. Eli and Shirah wanted nothing more than to participate in their relatives' joy, but without children of their own to hug, kiss, and cuddle, all they could do was cry, knowing that others couldn't fully understand their pain.

Today would be a very telling day. Eli and Shirah were scheduled to go to one of the biggest treatment centers in Manhattan, where they would undergo some very intense and grueling tests. The past few weeks had been particularly painful, and their hold on hope was slipping away by the minute. Reb Aron Shmuel called them beforehand to discuss the procedures with them;

instead of speaking on the phone, he asked if they could meet in person. They agreed, since they knew his easygoing nature would put their frayed nerves at ease.

Reb Aron Shmuel asked what they preferred to eat for lunch, extolling the virtues of various local restaurants. At this point, Eli could contain himself no longer, and he snapped, "Rabbi Jacobowitz, I don't want a tuna fish sandwich. I want a baby!" Eli was embarrassed that he had lost it, but felt vindicated in telling Rabbi Jacobowitz what he had told him. He thought to himself, *He must do this all the time and obviously lacks the sensitivity needed to understand my situation.*

There was a long pause on the other end of the line. Eli presumed that what he had told Rabbi Jacobowitz had struck a chord, but he was wrong. Reb Aron Shmuel's response will remain with Eli and Shirah. Eli later said it was unquestionably the biggest *chizuk* he ever received. "I just want you to understand that the *Ribbono Shel Olam* can give you a baby as easily as He can give you a tuna fish sandwich."

I was privileged to hear this story directly from Eli a few months before Shirah gave birth to a beautiful baby boy. Later, he shared it with the hundreds of people who attended the bris. Whether it is a baby for which we are longing, or any of the other blessings for which we hope and pray, we must always remember that the Ribbono Shel Olam can give it to us as easily as He can give us a sandwich.

Or on dry land as easily as on a cargo ship.

We just have to leave the how and the why to Him.

The Sleeping Stranger

The story of Chanukah is the story of a spark of light illuminating a world of darkness. This was true when the Chashmonaim defeated the Yevanim, and it has been true throughout the generations.

We all have moments of darkness, times when we struggle to find our way. Yet we have always been able to turn to the glimmering lights of the menorah to shed light and offer hope to the Jewish people in times of suffering. As we bask in the glow of those sacred candles, we can all lift ourselves from the doldrums and start anew.

Rav Simchah Levin, son of Rav Aryeh, the tzaddik of Yerushalayim, recounted a story that involved his father one Chanukah. Years later, the impression in his heart remained.

EVERY CHANUKAH, WHEN RAV ARYEH LEVIN LIT THE menorah, neighbors, family, and friends gathered around to observe as he recited the *berachos,* with fervor and warmth and passion. Placed in a rectangular glass case, the menorah was situated outside in the courtyard of his humble home, as is customary in Eretz Yisrael.

One Chanukah morning, Rav Aryeh arose at his normal time, a few hours before *neitz hachamah* (sunrise). As he walked out of his house, he noticed the strangest sight. A man was sleeping under the menorah case.

Rav Aryeh knew that the first order of business was waking up the man and bringing him inside. It was cold outside and the fellow, who reeked of liquor, seemed to be in a drunken stupor. At first, Rav Aryeh's attempts to wake him were unsuccessful; the man would not budge. Finally, he managed to shake him enough until he arose and stumbled toward the Levin home, eventually collapsing onto a wooden chair in the kitchen. Rav Aryeh made him a hot tea and tried his utmost to make the man feel comfortable. When Rav Aryeh felt the man was acclimated to his new surroundings, he gently asked, "Who are you? And what were you doing sleeping in our courtyard? Don't you have a home?"

The disheveled fellow looked into Rav Aryeh's warm and sympathetic eyes and shared his story.

I live all alone; I have no family. I have no way of supporting myself; my only means of support is through stealing. Last night, I was looking around for a house to rob and I chanced upon your home. From a distance, I saw a large crowd watching you light the menorah. I heard you make the berachos, listened as the crowd sang along, saw the joy on everyone's face. I remembered, if only for a moment, what Chanukah lighting was like in my childhood home when my father lit the menorah. And I said to myself, "How can I steal from these people? How can I steal from anyone?"

So I went home. When I got home, however, I grew lonely, depressed, and heartbroken. I searched the empty cabinets and found a bottle of arak. I opened it and began guzzling it down. But it wasn't enough. I wanted to capture that joy again, the joy I had experienced earlier that night. And so, I returned to your house, and as I came closer, I saw the lights were already extinguished. Even so, I felt the warmth I had experienced earlier. And even though the lights were no longer burning, I wanted to be as close as possible to the menorah. That's why I went to sleep right there, under the menorah.

Listening and empathizing, Rav Aryeh nodded and put his hand on the stranger's shoulder, giving him a comforting squeeze.

"I wish I could be happy like you," the man lamented. "Because I am sad, I drink. And then when I sober up, the sadness returns once more. It's a vicious cycle and I can't break it. Why do you and all those people look so happy while I'm so miserable? Please tell me."

Filled with compassion, Rav Aryeh explained, "You're sad because you're alone. But I'm not alone. I have a very rich Father Who takes very good care of me. He gives me everything I need. If He doesn't give me something, I know I don't need it. That's what makes me happy."

While his early morning guest sat in the kitchen sipping his tea, Rav Aryeh quoted the *pasuk, "Baruch hagever asher yivtach BaShem ve'hayah Hashem mivtacho* — Blessed is the man who trusts in Hashem, then Hashem will be his security" (*Yirmiyah* 17:7), and spoke more about *bitachon*. The whole discussion made a very strong impression on the sad and lonely individual.

Immediately, he accepted upon himself to completely refrain from drinking. Totally. Not a sip. And he kept to his word and was soon rehabilitated. In time, he became a *ben bayis* at Rav Aryeh's home, a member of the family. He lived out his days in joy, as a Torah-abiding Jew.

He had friends and a family.
And a Father taking care of him.
And that made him happy.

Just Another Shabbos Walk

For many years, I've been zocheh to serve as an eighth-grade rebbi in Yeshivas Chofetz Chaim-Talmudical Academy of Baltimore, located in its own neighborhood of Scotts Hill. The past few years, the yeshivah has hosted an eighth-grade Friday-

night mini-Shabbaton in the main Baltimore neighborhood — about a 10-minute drive from where I live near the school, though a very, very long walk. When this year's mini-Shabbaton was first arranged, I didn't plan on joining.

Then I found out that my co-rebbeim couldn't make it, and things began to shift; a new decision had to be made. Walking all alone for an hour and a half on a cold November Friday night is never an ideal proposition, especially considering that some of the neighborhoods I would be walking through were not exactly the safest. Neither my wife nor my principal thought I should do it. As of late Thursday afternoon, I was still not going. However, then my principal came up with an idea: a security guard to escort me the entire way. At first, it sounded ludicrous. But after seeing how serious he was about it, I discussed it with my wife, and I was on.

I thought back to a Shabbos some 35 years earlier, when I was learning in Telshe, Cleveland, and I had a sheva berachos to attend on Friday night in Wickliffe and a bar mitzvah Shabbos morning in Cleveland Heights. And I had to be at both. My good friend, Moshe Davis, accompanied me on the ten-mile, three-plus-hour walk through the snow. I don't think our feet touched the pavement the entire time.

Now, on that Friday in November, 2021, I called Moshe to let him know of my plans as we reminisced about that walk so many years ago. He reminded me that I was now 35 years older and should be a little more careful. He also told me that years earlier, when he was learning in Toronto, he had seen a Jew with a police escort on Rosh Hashanah. The man who received the escort was none other than Reb Moshe Reichmann.

So for one night, I would feel pretty important.

Of course, the rest of my friends and my family members teased me good-naturedly, claiming that one way or another, I would get a story out of the deal.

They weren't wrong.

BEFORE DRIVING TO THE SHUL WHERE THE *SEUDAH* WAS to take place, I put together my walking gear: ski hat (I planned to leave my Shabbos hat behind in the shul), gloves, two scarves. I also thought about the best way to use my time: counting my steps (minus the step counter on my phone, of course), *chazering* the Gemara I was teaching, or just plain thinking and making a *cheshbon hanefesh*. None of those plans panned out, though, until the second half of my walk.

As I drove to the shul, I thought about walking all the way back and wondered how I was going to make it. However, upon seeing the eager looks on the boys' faces when I arrived, I put those worries on the back burner. The davening was *leibedik* and warm, the Shabbos *seudah* everything we could have hoped for. The boys behaved beautifully, singing and dancing and listening to the speeches with true *derech eretz*. When *bentching* was over, after refusing the final offers from my fellow rebbeim to sleep in their homes, it was time to begin my journey.

My students were very excited that their rebbi was being honored with a security escort, and they danced me out the door. Then I went to meet Daryl, my personal bodyguard for the evening, who looked every bit the part. We weren't going anywhere near a war zone but if we would have, he was prepared. As I walked along the sidewalk, Daryl slowly drove alongside me on the road.

The wind was blowing and it was about 30°. No matter. Aside from being bundled up, the Shabbos wine in my system, along with the wonderful feeling that the Shabbaton had been a success, gave me a shot of adrenaline. For the first 5 to 10 minutes, I passed Yidden walking in the opposite direction. They seemed to know who I was, even though I wasn't wearing my Shabbos hat, and wished me a hearty *gut Shabbos*. Daryl was pleased with my popularity. I told him it was only because of him, my escort, that I was receiving any attention; his car's bright lights certainly drew attention in the quiet Jewish neighborhood. That extracted a chuckle.

There was still a long way to go.

I noticed that Daryl was not planning on watching me peripherally. Rather, he was going to escort me every step of the way. So as I kept walking — at three miles an hour, with Daryl sitting in his car at my side — we began to talk.

"Rabbi, can I ask you a question?"

"Sure," I responded.

"Why?" I wasn't sure what he meant, so I asked him to elaborate. "Why are you walking an hour and a half in the freezing weather when you can just get in the car, drive 10 minutes, and be there?"

I told him it was a good question and began to describe the concept of Shabbos: G-d created the world in six days and rested on the seventh. Just as He rested on the seventh day, we emulate Him and rest, too. I expounded, explaining that the Sabbath is the source of all blessing. If we guard it carefully, it will watch over us and we will be blessed.

"Cool!" was his excited response.

Now it was my turn. "Daryl, can I ask you a question?"

"Sure," he responded.

"Why?" This time, *he* wasn't sure what *I* meant and asked *me* to elaborate. "Why are you escorting a crazy rabbi who's walking in the cold? In other words, what made you become a security guard?"

At first, he was evasive, claiming he hadn't thought about it much, until I pushed a little further. "Tell me, was this your original dream in life?"

"Well, no," he admitted. "My dream was to become an Air Force pilot." Then, he shared his story, the story I had anticipated the moment I'd accepted this walk upon myself.

I went through years of training for special ops units, up to my last training jump. When it was time for that final jump, I found myself 45,000 feet in the air, along with a group of other trainees, in a C-17 Globemaster; the C-17 is used to deploy many troops at one time. I jumped out of that jet and landed a few minutes later.

I didn't hear it, but the others did. My knee had popped.

Somehow, I picked myself up off the ground and began to run the five kilometers (about three miles) to complete my mission. I don't remember anything after that. I collapsed and fainted. The next thing I knew, I was in a hospital. The doctor, who was not endowed with the best bedside manner, took a look at my chart and told me that I'd blown out my knee. He had no idea, he said, how I was able to run the five kilometers. He assured me, though, that I would have a brand-new knee by the next day. I'd be up and walking in no time at all.

And then he lowered the boom, delivering soul-crushing news in a matter-of-fact tone. "Your career in the Air Force is over." I couldn't believe it. Not only was my knee shattered but more importantly, my dreams had been shattered along with it.

I was sent home to recover, though I had no interest in doing anything. I holed myself up in my bedroom, where I lay in bed and sulked, completely depressed. One morning at 11 a.m., my father, a strong and stoic type, walked in and asked me in his deep voice, "Son, what are you doing?"

I couldn't bear to look at him, but I replied, "Dad, my dreams are over."

And my dad, who wasn't a big talker, countered, "Your dreams have only just begun."

He told me to look in the garage, and there it was: a 1985 Oldsmobile Cutlass. I may not have been able to fly a fighter jet. However, the old car was mine. I could work it over and make it into a really good drag-racing car.

And that's what I did, working on the car day and night. I put in a new engine and souped it up. And soon I began to race. Though the thrill of flying a fighter jet was the greatest thrill of my life, if I couldn't do that, this could also be an option. Drag racing became my hobby alongside my regular job in private security (the next logical choice after all my training), and it helped me make lots of extra money while enjoying some of the excitement I missed from the Air Force. I got married, had two kids who are my whole world, and managed to buy two beautiful houses.

"You know," Daryl continued as I huffed alongside him, "now that I think about it, I realize that if I would never have gotten hurt, I would have become a fighter pilot. It would have been nice and all that. However, two years later, some of my friends were deployed to Afghanistan and never returned. So I guess you could say it all worked out for the best."

I was very much taken by Daryl's story and said to him, "Daryl, now let's connect the dots. G-d wanted you to escort a rabbi on his Sabbath walk. In order to get there, you had to take a roundabout journey. And now, here we are together. Your dreams have been realized. You have a family and two lovely homes. It's just not the route you thought you had to take to get here." Daryl shook his head in disbelief. I, too, thought it was remarkable.

By this point, I had reached the halfway mark; I was 45 minutes into my walk. For the rest of my trek, I pretty much kept to myself, while Daryl continued to drive alongside me at three miles an hour. When I told him he didn't have to stay right next to me, he said it was his honor and privilege, and he remained at my side until I reached my house.

When I finally made it, I thanked him for a very enjoyable trip, stating that maybe one day we will meet up again. Then we parted ways.

I was glad to be back home and enjoyed the rest of Shabbos with my family. When I told them all about my walk, they couldn't help but laugh. As always, I had somehow found a story along the way.

I learned many lessons that Friday night. First, I learned how secure it felt to receive a security escort. As Daryl traveled alongside me, I tried to contemplate how Hashem provides us with so much more protection and cares for our every need. And He's not just there for an hour-and-a-half walk. He's there for our entire lives.

I also learned that even though it took me an hour and a half, much longer than a 10-minute car ride, when you have to work hard for something, even if it means walking through the cold and aching all over, in the end you appreciate it more. This is true with every journey of our lives. If it takes longer to reach our destination, and there are more challenges along the way, the goal becomes more valuable.

Last, I learned that even though we don't understand why things happen the way they do, there is always a reason. Sometimes we will connect the dots, and sometimes we won't. Yet if we trust in Him, we'll know that this is where we were meant to be.

TESHUVAH

The Wheel of Fortune

Rav Mordechai Neugroschel, a well-known speaker in Eretz Yisrael, shared a story that carries many powerful lessons. Perhaps most of all, it reminds us how the wheel of life goes round and round. And when we help another, we are really helping ourselves.

ABOUT 30 YEARS AGO, DONI WAS LEARNING IN A YESHIVAH in Eretz Yisrael and putting in less than stellar effort. His rebbeim spoke to him numerous times, but he continued to slack off. They warned him repeatedly that if he doesn't improve, he is going to earn himself a ticket to another yeshivah. Still, he ignored their threats and kept on performing poorly.

One day, after cutting *seder* yet again, Doni found an envelope waiting in his dormitory room. Though it was addressed to his parents, he was fairly certain of its contents. To confirm his suspicions, he opened the envelope and read the official letter, which informed his parents that Doni would not be allowed back into the yeshivah for the next *zman*.

Obviously, the yeshivah did not do this in the most responsible way. It would have been much better if they had invited Doni's parents to the yeshivah and given them the upsetting news in person. But they didn't. And now, he had to give the letter to his parents.

He knew they were disappointed with his behavior and he didn't want to face the reality, so he devised a plan.

Instead of passing the letter on to his parents, he ripped it up. That's right. If his parents never received a letter, he could pretend he had not seen it either. It was a risky plan but he felt it was the best way to obtain yet another chance.

The next *zman*, Doni walked in to yeshivah as if nothing had ever happened. The first day, the *menahel* called him over and asked why he was there. Doni pulled his best innocent face and asked why he wouldn't be back. The *menahel* pressed him about the letter, but he did his best "deer in the headlights" pretense, acting as if this were the first time he was ever hearing about it. The *menahel* wasn't going for it, and the discussion soon turned heated.

Walking by was Reb Nachum Gold, an American *yungerman* who had joined the yeshivah within the past year. Though he and his wife had begun married life in America, when almost five years had passed and they hadn't yet been blessed with children, it was recommended that they move to Eretz Yisrael. Perhaps a change of place would help tear up their decree of childlessness (see *Rosh Hashanah* 16b).

As soon as Reb Nachum overheard the exchange between Doni and the *menahel,* he made an offer to the *menahel,* with whom he enjoyed an excellent rapport. If the *hanhalah* allowed Doni to stay, he, Reb Nachum, would learn with him and take him under his wing. The *menahel* promised to get back to Reb Nachum later that day, and after meeting with his fellow *hanhalah* members, he decided to give it a shot.

Reb Nachum and Doni hit it off. Doni began performing like he was capable of performing and learning with *hasmadah. Chazering* a *shiur* he now understood, thanks to Reb Nachum, made all the difference in the world.

Not only did Doni improve drastically, but Reb Nachum and his wife were soon blessed with a son. Their *yeshuos* seemed intertwined. Reb Nachum had infused life into an almost lifeless *bachur,* and he and his wife were blessed with the gift of a new life, a baby boy. What a story!

But our story is just beginning.

Doni continued his ascent and made the yeshivah ever so proud. He became one of the stars of the yeshivah, one of the most well-liked *bachurim.* He did especially well with the younger boys who were struggling as he had. He learned with them and spoke to them about their issues, encouraging and motivating each one. He told them he had experienced similar issues when he was younger, and he had overcome them to get where he was. After Doni got married, he learned in kollel and was eventually hired to work in a yeshivah with boys who were looking to find themselves.

One day, a boy with a backpack and hair to his shoulders entered the building and introduced himself as Rocky. Though he came from a frum home and all of his brothers and sisters were very typical, frum kids, Rocky was the black sheep of the family and his parents had trouble connecting to him. At this point in his struggles, he wanted to find out what life was really about and was planning on backpacking through Asia. He was just making a quick stop in Israel. Doni heard Rocky out, welcomed him warmly, and offered him a place to stay for a few days before continuing his journey.

Those few days made a huge impact on Rocky. He decided to stay in yeshivah, where he developed a very close relationship with Doni, becoming a *ben bayis* in his home. As time passed, Rocky became a serious *ben Torah,* making an amazing turnaround. A few years down the line, Doni and his wife set up Rocky, or Yerachmiel as he was called once again, with a wonderful girl who had a similar life story. The two of them began to date and a few weeks later, they were engaged.

As Yerachmiel transformed himself, he constantly expressed concern that were he to go home, he might fall back into his previous lifestyle and unhealthy behavior. Understanding where his worries were coming from, his parents encouraged him to stay as long as he felt was necessary.

Now, however, his parents were traveling in for his wedding, and they would be reunited with their son. The last time they had seen each other, they were barely on speaking terms. Though over the phone, the relationship had improved now that Yerachmiel had made his way back, he had more than a little bit of anxiety about seeing his parents in person. Doni reassured his *talmid* and told him he would be there for him.

Yerachmiel's parents flew in during the week of the wedding, and he went to greet them at the airport; there were many hugs and tears. All in all, the meeting went very well. The day of the wedding, Yerachmiel's parents were getting ready at the wedding hall when Doni, Yerachmiel's beloved rebbi and mentor, walked in.

Suddenly, Yerachmiel's father's eyes lit up and he ran over to Doni and the two embraced.

It was Reb Nachum — he was Yerachmiel's father!

Many years had passed since he and Doni had last seen each other. After their first child was born, Reb Nachum and his wife had returned to America and had another five children. Their oldest son, though, had a very difficult time and struggled with Yiddishkeit. Although Reb Nachum had seen such success with other kids like Yerachmiel, he couldn't find common ground with his own son, who decided to backpack through Asia, with a quick stop in Israel.

And the rest, as they say, is history.
The wheel had come full circle.
Ve'heishiv lev avos al banim.

The Holy Thief

There are times when people walk into the homes of the greatest Torah leaders of our times with unusual requests. Rav Aharon Leib Shteinman, the gadol hador, was no exception; he received his fair share of strange questions and petitions, which, for the most part, he granted. At times, the requests bordered on the ridiculous, yet Rav Aharon Leib obliged those petitioners, as well — whenever feasible, that is.

A MAN ONCE ENTERED THE HUMBLE AND SPARSELY FURnished home of Rav Aharon Leib and asked for one "simple" favor. "Rebbi, I'd like to sit next to you in Gan Eden."

While the others standing around the rosh yeshivah stood with mouths agape, Rav Aharon Leib immediately responded, "Gan Eden? Who says I'm going to gain entry into Gan Eden?"

This was not the response the fellow had anticipated. He was hoping for a *berachah* or perhaps some *chizuk*. Fumbling over his words, he asked, "Why wouldn't the rosh yeshivah go to Gan Eden?"

Rav Aharon Leib's reply surprised those within earshot. "Because I'm a *ganav;* that's why I won't go to Gan Eden."

"A *ganav*? When? How? Where?" This was quickly becoming more than the visitor had bargained for.

Rav Aharon Leib continued, "Not once, but twice I was a *ganav.* And that's why I don't know if I will gain entry into Gan Eden."

With that, Rav Aharon Leib began his first tale of thievery. "It was between the two world wars and I was just a young boy. I wanted to communicate with my family, but I was unable to do so. I decided to write them a letter, yet I had a problem. I was so poor that I didn't even have enough money for one stamp. Though it was only a few pennies, the smallest amount of currency, I didn't have even that. I went to the post office and asked the clerk if I could mail the letter anyway. I figured that if the letter would reach its destination, I would pay the post office for the service after the fact. Sure enough, the letter reached my family, who sent me some money. Now I had enough money to pay for a stamp. However, there was one problem. The country had dissolved; it was disbanded completely and no longer existed. There was no one to pay, so I never reimbursed the country for the stamp. You see, I'm a *ganav*."

Stunned at the purity and innocence of the rosh yeshivah, no one said a word. But Rav Aharon Leib was not finished yet. There was a second incident to share. "On another occasion, I was walking by a garden and I plucked a beautiful flower. I don't remember whose garden it was, so I can't pay them back. As you can see, I'm a *ganav noch a mohl* (again)."

While the first story was incredible, it also seemed more credible. A young boy with no money sent a letter and had no way to repay the minuscule price of a stamp. But the second story seemed strange. Rav Aharon Leib, the *gadol hador,* was walking by a garden and plucked a flower? And he didn't remember where it all happened? Something seemed to be missing.

Curious as to what the real story was, the fellow who initially made the request of Rav Aharon Leib about being his neighbor in Gan Eden asked Rav Aharon Leib's daughter to clarify the second story, to perhaps fill in the missing details. When he recounted Rav Aharon Leib's version, his daughter smiled. Yes, the story was true, and yes, her father had left out a few crucial details, so she filled them in:

"My little daughter was walking by a scenic garden and plucked a pretty flower. When she brought it to me, I commented on how lovely it was and she was so proud of herself. But when I asked her where she got the flower from, explaining that the Torah does not allow picking flowers from another's garden, her entire mood changed and she became distressed. She hemmed and hawed and finally admitted that she'd plucked it without thinking and didn't remember where it had come from. Soon enough, she grew hysterical and started crying uncontrollably at the thought that she was now saddled with sin, unable to right her wrong. I tried to explain that it was all right, it was an accident, but she wouldn't calm down. I decided to bring her to my father. He would be able to find the proper words to help her feel better.

"But when I brought her over to my father and explained the entire story, she continued to carry on. That is, until my father told her that he would take the *aveirah* of stealing on his shoulders. As soon as she heard that, she calmed down. She was no longer terrified of the ramifications of her action."

Thus, the second time in which Rav Aharon Leib was a "*ganav*" had nothing to do with him, but was merely an innocent mistake of his granddaughter's, which he had taken upon his shoulders to put her at ease.

Perhaps we can understand this story as a mashal for the teshuvah process. There are times when we recognize the enormity of our sins and we become overwhelmed. We want, in the deepest recesses of our hearts, to right our wrongs, to be clean and pure and innocent again. At that moment, when we sincerely regret our mistakes and perhaps even shed a tear, the Al-mighty provides us with an opportunity to unburden ourselves of our aveiros, to take those sins off of our shoulders, allowing us to be free once again!

A Knock at the Door

Yossel Polluch was special from the moment he was born. He was one of those children who did everything right.

Pure. Untainted. Holy.

Throughout his time here on earth, a short 54 years, Reb Yossel utilized every moment to serve Hashem. He just wanted to learn and to teach and to help others come close to the Almighty.

After he passed away, a man walked into the shivah home and told an amazing story, which shows how Reb Yossel's will to serve and teach saved lives. Literally.

AFTER HIS MARRIAGE, REB YOSSEL MOVED TO TEL AVIV, where he became part of the Gerrer *kehillah* in that city and taught Torah. It was never anything formal. He would come every day to shul and would teach those who were there. It didn't matter what. Whatever they wanted to learn, he was willing to teach. Then one day, there was a torrential downpour, the type of unforgiving rain one often encounters in the winter in Eretz Yisrael.

Reb Yossel entered the *beis midrash* but no one was there. He waited for someone to come so he could learn with them. Yet the clock was ticking, time was passing, and still no one had arrived. Finally, Reb Yossel decided to take matters into his own hands. He figured if no one was coming in, he would go outside and recruit them. He walked outside the building and into the driving rainstorm. Yet as the wind blew and the rain poured down, no one even stopped to listen to what he had to say. Everyone was just trying to get from one place to another. Certainly in a secular environment, nobody was going to stop what they were doing to learn Torah!

Even so, Reb Yossel wanted to teach. He was bursting to learn Torah with someone. Anyone.

Well, if he couldn't find anyone on the street, he would walk into the closest apartment building and knock on the door of the first-floor apartment, to invite the individual who lived there to come learn with him. No sooner said than done. He crossed the street, entered the apartment building right there, walked up to the door, and began to knock. When no one answered, he knocked with a little more persistence. Still no answer.

As his desperation grew, he decided once more to go back out onto the street and try his luck. This time, too, nobody gave him the time of day. With umbrellas in one hand and cell phones in the other, the passersby didn't even notice he was trying to communicate with them.

Reb Yossel was determined to try once more to recruit someone from the ground-floor apartment, so he entered the building and knocked on the door of the first-floor apartment yet again. This time, though, it was more like a bang. He waited a bit and banged again.

Finally, the door opened. Standing in front of him was a disheveled-looking man in his 30s, with long hair and bloodshot eyes. He looked like he had awoken from a deep, deep slumber.

Now that someone had finally answered, Reb Yossel was not sure what to say, so he said it straight. "Would you like to learn with me?"

With a look of agitation in his eyes, the man snapped, "Who sent you? Who wants to know?"

Now Reb Yossel really didn't know what to say. As he hesitated, the apartment owner had more time to react. He grabbed Reb Yossel by the lapels and repeated, "Who wants to know? Who sent you?"

Taken aback, Reb Yossel eked out a response. "Hashem sent me."

Realizing he had overreacted, the man let go of Reb Yossel and asked if he could tell his story. Reb Yossel, *tzaddik* that he was, readily agreed.

"Ever since I was a little boy, I fought with my parents about Yiddishkeit. By the time I was a teenager, I decided to go off on my own. They tried to reach out to me and to keep me in the fold, but I didn't want that type of lifestyle and didn't want anybody bothering me about it. So I cut off ties with my family, and for the last 20 years I've been on my own. In truth, I'm miserable. I can't hold down a job, I have no friends, and I have no connection to anyone at all. Today, I concluded: No more! I was going to end my life."

To prove his point, the man invited Reb Yossel into his bedroom and showed him the noose hanging from a beam.

"First, though, I had a last-minute conversation with G-d. I gave Him one last chance and told Him that if he really wants me, He should send me a sign. At that moment, there was a knock at the door. At first, I thought my mind was playing tricks on me. However, after the knocking continued, I stepped off of the stool and walked toward the door. But when I opened it, there was no one there. So I went back to finish the job.

"As soon as I got back to my bedroom, though, the knocking started up again. This time, it was much louder. When I answered the door, you were standing there. I was so shocked that I grabbed you and asked who sent you..."

The man was visibly shaken. Reb Yossel held his hand and invited him once more to learn, as a way of calming him down and developing a relationship. Reb Yossel encouraged him, helped to build him up, and ultimately helped heal him. With time, the man returned to his roots and became healthy enough to marry and build a family of his own.

At this point in the telling of the story, the man sitting in the Polluch home looked around. His voice turned quiet.

"I am that man."

And he began to cry, overwhelmed by the kindness and warmth

that had saved his life.

The Polluch children knew their father was special.

This was just one more example.

His sincere and strong desire to teach Torah to another Jew and bring him closer to Hashem had saved generations.

Saving Your Own

At times, when a child from a secular home chooses to become religious, his parents feel as if they've lost him. This child, whom they nurtured and cared for, won't eat their food and won't socialize in their circles, causing his parents to feel inferior, leading to much anger and aggravation. Though kiruv professionals emphasize to their students the importance of treading carefully and speaking respectfully to their parents, the newly minted baalei teshuvah may have trouble following their advice, which often triggers much conflict. Parents have even formed support groups where they share the frustration, hurt, and indignation against their children who've figuratively slapped them in the face and turned their backs on their way of life. But it doesn't stop there. These parents may resort to irrational behavior, as they take out their frustration against those who "brainwashed" their children. Rav Yosef Wallis, the founder of Arachim, a powerful kiruv organization in Eretz Yisrael, is frequently the recipient of such backlash.

ONE DAY, RAV WALLIS RECEIVED AN ANGRY PHONE CALL from one such mother, who demanded that he come and speak to her immediately. She complained bitterly, "My daughter doesn't listen to a word I say and it's all your fault.

Give me back my old daughter, the one who had some respect for me."

The woman couldn't have called at a worse time. It was Erev Pesach and Rav Wallis was in the supermarket with a shopping cart "filled to the sky." He had been waiting in line for 20 minutes, and he was finally ready to unload his groceries for checkout when the call came in. But he knew he didn't have much of a choice. If he refused to come and see the woman, the relationship with her daughter could deteriorate further. So he left his shopping cart and told the woman he would meet her in 15 minutes.

As soon as the woman answered the door, she began screaming at him, complaining about her daughter who was disrespectful and impertinent. As she let off steam, Rav Yosef noticed the daughter she was speaking about sitting in the corner of the room with a defiant look on her face. Rav Yosef asked the young woman, "Don't you know that *kibbud eim* is a *mitzvah d'Oraisa*? You have to respect your mother and you have to listen to what she says. If you have a difference of opinion, then you work it out, but always in a respectful manner. Obviously, if your mother tells you to do something that is entirely against the rules of the Torah, then you can't listen to her. Yet even that doesn't give you the right to disrespect her."

The daughter then told her side of the story, and Rav Yosef became the mediator for the evening. Although he had so much to do, he knew how important it was for him to stay and listen and intervene as each one of them aired their grievances. By the time the evening had come to an end, it seemed that the daughter and mother had made peace with each other. The mother apologized for getting so upset and taking it out on Rav Wallis. He reassured her that it wasn't a problem and wished them both a good Yom Tov.

Many years passed. Rav Yosef's newborn grandson came down with fever and had to be rushed to Mayanei Hayeshua Medical Center. After a slew of blood tests, X-rays, and a spinal tap, the doctors ruled out almost every illness except bacterial meningitis. If not treated immediately, meningitis in infants can cause extensive damage, even death. As such, even before confirming the positive results, the head nurse, an Orthodox woman, suggested that antibiotics be administered ASAP. After receiving permission from the doctors, she hooked the baby up to an IV and began the antibiotics. Then she suggested that he be transferred to Beilinson Hospital, where they were better equipped to deal with pediatric meningitis, and she arranged the transfer. The family expressed their gratitude to the head nurse for all of her assistance. Soon after their arrival at Beilinson, the diagnosis was confirmed; the baby had bacterial meningitis. Thankfully, he had already received the first dose of the lifesaving antibiotic and was already on the road to recovery.

A few months later, the child made a full recovery, and the family planned a *seudas hodaah*, where they would all recite *Nishmas*. Aside from family and close friends, they invited the medical providers who had been involved in the baby's care from both hospitals. Overjoyed that the baby had recovered, the head nurse from Mayanei Hayeshua agreed to join the celebration. But when she walked into the house and saw Rav Yosef Wallis, she stopped abruptly.

Taking note of her hesitancy, Rav Yosef asked if everything was all right.

She looked him in the eye and said, "You don't recognize me, do you?"

Rav Yosef meets thousands of people a year, and he can't recognize all of them years later. However, he didn't want to insult her for having forgotten her, so he paused, trying to place the woman. She quickly came to his rescue. "About 15 years ago, my daughter decided to become Torah observant and was giving me lots of aggravation. I called you in a panic on Erev Pesach, and you dropped everything and immediately came to mediate our differences. So what can I say? Not only did she become fully observant, but she took me along for the ride.

"Soon after, I wanted a more religious atmosphere in the workplace, and I transferred from my post in Ichilov to Mayanei Hayeshua, where your grandson was brought in that traumatic evening a few months ago. Had you not come and made peace that night 15 years ago, who knows how things would have played out? There's a strong possibility that I would never have made it to Mayanei Hayeshua, and I would not have had the opportunity to help save your grandson."

There was a reason Rav Wallis didn't recognize the head nurse. With her head covered, she looked like any other observant woman, nothing like the furious, anti-religious mother of so many years ago.

Rav Wallis later reflected: On Erev Pesach 15 years ago, he'd thought he was dropping everything to save the day in the home of a young baalas teshuvah, when in essence, he was dropping everything to save his very own grandson.

Very Good Inside

Rebbes are very busy.

With hundreds, even thousands, of Chassidim and numerous responsibilities, they often have little to no time left, even for simchos. As such, they cannot attend every chasunah they are invited to, let alone each l'chaim, tenaim, or sheva berachos, even for Chassidim.

But sometimes, there are exceptions to the rule.

A MAN IN HIS MID-60S ONCE WENT TO THE BOBOVER Rebbe, Rav Shlomo Halberstam, and invited the Rebbe to his youngest daughter's *sheva berachos*. It seemed like an unusual request. It was well-known that the Rebbe had a very hectic schedule, which left little time for attending *simchos,* and the man wasn't even a Bobover Chassid. Why would the Rebbe attend this *sheva berachos*?

But something in the man's tone intrigued the Rebbe; he sensed it was important for him to go, so he agreed. The Rebbe walked into the *simchah* and immediately the *baal simchah* ran over to welcome him. "Rebbe, I must tell you my story," and he proceeded to reveal the story behind his strong desire to have the Rebbe at the *sheva berachos.*

> *Though I was only a young man before the war, Hashem blessed me with a melodious voice and I served as a chazzan in Bobov. People seemed to enjoy when I davened for the amud.*
>
> *Then the Nazis arrived and I lost everything. My entire family was destroyed. My wife and children were taken from me, along with my friends and just about everyone I knew. I was utterly alone.*
>
> *To be quite honest with you, my faith was terribly shaken. I had questions with no answers. And so, one Shabbos shortly after the war, feeling completely lost, I pulled out a cigarette and smoked. It felt very strange but I was very angry and very upset. It's not so much that I needed or wanted the cigarette, I just didn't want to keep Shabbos.*
>
> *One Shabbos, after you and your son finished davening in your newly established shtiebel, the two of you passed me on your way home. You could have ignored me and walked the other way, but you turned to me warmly and said, "You used to be a chazzan in the town of Bobov. Why don't you come to our shtiebel? I'm sure the olam would love to hear you daven once more for the amud!" I tried my hardest to refuse, but*

with your warmth and sincerity, you convinced me.

The next week, I made my way to the shtiebel, where I davened for the amud. After davening, you thanked me, praising my davening effusively and repeatedly, making me feel so good about it.

But I was still a mechallel Shabbos.

The next Shabbos, the two of you passed me again. This time, though, when you came by, I was in the midst of smoking my cigarette. Even so, you didn't look at me in a disapproving manner. You didn't chide me. You didn't say one word about my smoking. Instead, you told me, "Last Shabbos, you gave us such hana'ah (enjoyment) when you davened fahren amud (in front of the amud). Would you do us the favor once more this Shabbos?" I was very taken with the offer.

But your son looked at you quizzically and stated, "Tatte, he's a mechallel Shabbos! Are we really going to bring a mechallel Shabbos to Bobov to daven fahren amud?"

I stood there not knowing what to say. He was right.

However, you responded, "He is not a mechallel Shabbos. It's the Hitler inside of him that is mechallel Shabbos."

So I came back to shul to daven for the amud. After davening, you complimented me once more. As I was about to leave, you asked me to stay for Kiddush. I did.

Slowly, my life began to turn around.

"Today," concluded the *baal simchah,* "I am a *shomer Torah u'mitzvos,* no different from other frum Yidden. *Baruch Hashem,* I have been blessed with a large family, all *shomrei Torah u'mitzvos*. That came about only because you looked in my heart and saw that I did not mean to be a *mechallel Shabbos*. It was only a result of the hopelessness the Nazis planted inside of me. Once you showed me who I really was, I was able to become that person once again."

Sometimes, an individual finds himself in a very bad place. Perhaps he's going through a crisis of some sort, whether physical, financial, emotional, or spiritual, making him feel upset and somewhat disillusioned, not permitting him to perform at his best.

However, a Yid must know that he is innately good; he has such goodness inside of him. Only the crisis and difficulty are causing him to sin.

Chazal tell us, "Ein adam over aveirah ella im kein nichnas bo ruach shtus — A person only commits a transgression if a spirit of foolishness enters him" (Sotah 3a).

Perhaps that's the message. A person must separate himself from his sin.

When he does, he is able to realize how very good he is — and how very great he can be.

MITZVOS

To Make His Neshamah Shine

SHORTLY AFTER THE PASSING OF RAV NOACH OF LECHOvitch, his *talmid*, Rav Avraham Weinberg, founded the Slonimer Chassidus. Rav Avraham, the author of *Yesod HaAvodah*, was eager to infuse other Yidden with *dveikus* and feelings of closeness to Hashem; he therefore made himself available to anyone who wanted to meet with him and seek his guidance and blessings. Especially over Yom Tov, many Chassidim flocked to Slonim to receive a *berachah* from the Rebbe while they wished him a *gut Yom Tov*.

During this era, Jews were often drafted into the national armies and could be found in the Polish, Hungarian, Lithuanian, Russian, and German armies, where they were subject to continuous persecution and open hatred. At best, they were taunted and bullied but at times, it was much worse. And so, an opportunity to receive a blessing was a welcome one. Often, if a soldier was stationed near any Rebbe, he took advantage and made his way to that Rebbe for a *berachah*.

Among those who visited the Slonimer Rebbe one Succos was Pavel, a Jewish soldier stationed in the region. He was happy to get away for a short while and receive a much-needed *berachah*, before heading out to yet another battle with both the enemy from within as well as the enemy from without, the opposing armies who occasionally threatened their neighbors.

On the first day of Succos, as guests visited the Rebbe's *succah*, he offered words of wisdom and encouragement to each one, to help deal with the various ailments and tribulations they faced. When Pavel arrived, however, the Rebbe looked up, intrigued. This was not just any soldier. Although the Rebbe praised all those who displayed *mesirus nefesh* to hold onto their Yiddishkeit, he could sense that Pavel had something special about him. An aura, a glow, emanated from his face, and, in a much deeper sense, from his *neshamah*.

The Rebbe was determined to discover this young man's secret. "Tell me, what mitzvah did you perform recently to allow your *neshamah* to shine in such a manner?"

Pavel smiled. He wasn't a particularly learned individual; he didn't spend his days and nights immersed in Torah study and prayer. He was just a soldier. But last night had been special. He hadn't told anyone what had taken place, and he didn't know how the Rebbe knew. But somehow he did.

Now, he revealed his secret.

> *We are not currently at war and there is no danger in the immediate area. Nevertheless, every night a soldier stands guard. Rebbe, last night was my night; I had to stand at my post from dusk to dawn. I couldn't get away for even a moment. I paced back and forth, gun in hand, looking and listening for anything amiss.*
>
> *But as the time passed slowly there in the cold, I noticed a small hut, a succah, perhaps a thousand feet from where I stood guard. A lantern glowed from the inside and beckoned me to come. Never in my life have I wanted so badly to participate in the mitzvah of succah. But I couldn't leave my post.*
>
> *A group of gruff soldiers sat nearby; they have no love for*

me and were certainly not candidates to take over for me for a few moments. Since they were right there, drinking and playing cards and getting more and more inebriated by the minute, they could easily report me were I to leave my post, even though there was no inherent danger.

The clock was ticking and the hours passed. Chatzos was drawing nearer by the moment, and my opportunity to make the berachah of Leisheiv BaSuccah on the first night of Succos was fading quickly (see Orach Chaim 639). Finally, 15 minutes before midnight, without any warning, the soldiers stood up and walked away. The coast was clear, if only for a few moments. I dashed toward the succah with a piece of bread in my hand. After running a bit and then climbing a fence, I was finally inside. Rebbe, you cannot imagine my anticipation and excitement. I washed my hands, pulled out the bread, and made the berachah of HaMotzi and then Leisheiv BaSuccah. A few minutes later, I bentched and ran back to where I was standing. It was an unbelievable feeling to have accomplished something I never thought would happen. Thankfully, no one noticed I was gone.

"Rebbe," Pavel concluded, "I was *zocheh* to fulfill the mitzvah. I imagine that's what the Rebbe sensed. Had someone noticed I was missing, the consequences would have been severe. In essence, I risked my life for the performance of the mitzvah."

The Rebbe complimented Pavel on his sacrifice and devotion. "It is quite admirable that you risked so much for the performance of the mitzvah. You will receive enormous reward for your efforts. Yet even though you sacrificed a great deal, there was something even more that caused your *neshamah* to shine like this. What else did you do?"

Pavel was surprised. Certainly that had been his most prominent deed of the night. What could the Rebbe be referring to? He thought and thought and then a grin formed on his face.

"Rebbe, I think I know. When I came back to my post, I was so delighted that I had been granted the opportunity and privilege to perform the mitzvah that I could not help but sing and dance the rest of the night."

The Rebbe smiled. Pavel smiled.

Ashreinu mah tov chelkeinu!

Bankruptcy and Blessings

One of the holiest figures of the last generation was the Sephardic mekubal, Rav Yisrael Abuchatzeira, better known as the Baba Sali. From his humble home in Netivot, the Baba Sali orchestrated one unlikely yeshuah after another. There are numerous stories of the miracles he performed.

While this story is also in many ways miraculous, it also carries with it a very practical and down-to-earth message, the combination of which makes the narrative most meaningful.

AFTER ARRANGING AN APPOINTMENT TO MEET WITH the Sephardic *mekubal,* a non-observant paraplegic paid a visit to Baba Sali. Though he had seen many doctors and had been told he would never walk again, the man entered the home of Baba Sali with one request. "Please help me get better."

Baba Sali asked him three questions. To his credit, the man's replies were straightforward and truthful.

"Do you keep Shabbat?"

"No, I don't keep Shabbat."

Baba Sali then asked him another pointed question. "Do you put on *tefillin* every day?"

Again, the answer was no.

When Baba Sali asked him if he learns Torah, the man could only shake his head in the negative.

The Sephardic sage countered sharply, "So how can you possibly ask me for a *berachah* that you should be healed? Upon what should that blessing rest? In order for a blessing to work, you need to have a *kli*, a vessel fit for a blessing, a receptacle to hold the *berachah*. Only if one observes the Torah can blessings be effective. And you don't."

Immediately, the fellow promised to accept upon himself to observe those three mitzvos: Shabbat, *tefillin,* and *limud Torah.*

Baba Sali sensed the seriousness of the man's response and cast his gaze upon him. "I command you, get up and walk!"

Trembling, the man held onto both sides of his wheelchair and with trepidation, lifted himself out of the wheelchair and slowly stood up. It was truly a miracle. But Baba Sali was not yet satisfied. "*Rutz*, run!"

The man slowly placed one foot in front of the other and began to walk. After a few steps, he became more and more comfortable and steadier, and picked up his pace. Before long, he was running. He was so elated that he ran all the way to Yeshivat HaNegev, also in Netivot. The moment the door opened, those who recognized him jumped out of their seats and began singing and dancing. Soon, the circle grew and an indescribable joy flooded the room.

Word spread rather quickly.

But that's not where the story ends.

The rosh yeshivah of Yeshivat HaNegev was the renowned *marbitz Torah* and *gaon*, Rav Yissachar Meir. He attracted many young men who did not grow up in Torah-oriented homes; under his tutelage and guidance, they became true *bnei Torah* and *talmidei chachamim.*

That night, under the thick veil of darkness, long after most had gone to sleep, there was a knock at Rav Yissachar's door. Rav Yissachar, who was sitting at his dining-room table learning, stood up to answer it.

There stood Baba Sali.

This had never happened before. At first, Rav Yissachar didn't know what to do. "*Kvod harav,* why did you have to come visit me in middle of the night? What is so urgent? I could have come to your home!"

But Baba Sali paid no attention. *Kavod* meant nothing to him.

"Today, I lost all of my *Olam Haba,*" he stated plainly, with more than a tinge of sadness. "My entire life I've worked to accumulate mitzvot; each one enhanced my *cheilek* in *Olam Haba*. It was all on one condition — the mitzvah had to be performed without any publicity. For this reason, the moment the miracle that occurred today became publicized, I lost everything. The honor and fame emptied my portion and left me bankrupt in *Olam Haba*. All my *zechuyot* are gone!

"Fame diminishes merits. The more fame, the less reward. Imagine a bus card. Every moment of publicity punches a hole in it, and a large amount of publicity empties the card entirely. So my card is now empty. I need to begin anew; I need to start saving up again.

"Which is why I came to you. You have a wonderful yeshivah filled with *bnei yeshivah* who learn with *hatmadah* and sacrifice themselves for Torah. I emptied my savings from my bank account in this world to build up my savings in *Olam Haba*. I'd like to give you all my money, tens of thousands of dollars, for the learning in the yeshivah. Please take the money so I can build my house in *Olam Haba*." With that, he handed a thick wad of cash to Rav Yissachar.

On one condition.

No one was to know.

And no one knew until the Baba Sali passed away.

No, Smarty Pants

We live in a world where we take the basics for granted. We expect kosher food, the ability to keep Shabbos, and endless opportunities for mitzvos and chesed. But it wasn't always this way, and we must appreciate the sacrifice and commitment of those who preceded us.

For it is upon their shoulders that we stand.

The following story, told by Rav Chizkiyahu Karelenstein, speaks of such sacrifice and commitment, and also of the power and wisdom of the Jewish woman.

IN THE EARLY 1900S, TWO GOOD FRIENDS, MOSHE AND Chaim, enjoyed a simple life in Radin, in the vicinity of the Chofetz Chaim and other Torah giants. But the poverty was stifling and they dreamed of bigger and better. After hearing that the streets of America were lined with gold, they determined that the time had come to unearth its treasures.

Many warned them that they were sacrificing the spiritual future of their families, but they assured the doomsayers that they would give up nothing. Their commitment to Torah and mitzvos and Shabbos was not negotiable. They merely sought a chance at success and financial freedom.

Much easier said than done. The temptations were many.

Moshe and Chaim and their families arrived in America, with wide-eyed excitement and abundant hope of achieving financial success rather quickly. But jobs were not easy to come by, and not easy to hold onto. Every Friday, at the end of a long workweek, the foreman of their current factory would tell them, "See you tomorrow."

And every single week, their response was the same as the week before: "We cannot work on Saturday. Our Sabbath is not negotiable."

And every single week, the foreman's response echoed the response of the other foremen they had worked for: "Come to work on Saturday, or don't bother coming back on Monday."

And every Monday, after staying home on Shabbos and celebrating with their families, they went to look for a new job.

It was deflating to have to begin the job search again every week. Even so, Moshe and Chaim proved resilient. Their families, while hungry, were proud of the iron determination their fathers showed. Slowly, though, over time, the weekly indignation and frustration began to take their toll; the continual strain was wearing Moshe and Chaim down.

Until one day, when their fortune took a turn for the better.

Moshe and Chaim both landed jobs in an insurance company, with good pay and a reasonable schedule. When the first Friday arrived, they braced for the inevitable. This time, however, when they explained that Saturday was non-negotiable, the supervisor's response was surprising. "I don't care how you get your work done. If you can get it done by Friday, then you can take off on your Sabbath. Otherwise, you better be here on Saturday." Ecstatic with the new arrangement, Moshe and Chaim ran home to share the good news with their families. They could go back to their jobs on Monday, without looking for a new one.

This went on for a few months. But then World War I arrived and the attitude changed. The United States was at war, and in the words of the supervisor, "We need all hands on deck." Which meant on Shabbos, too. When Moshe and Chaim protested, the supervisor, who had always been kind and sympathetic, turned hard-nosed and stubborn and gave them an ultimatum. "If you don't want to agree to the new conditions and show up every Saturday, then pack up your stuff and go home."

Chaim, although disappointed, told himself that he had been

through the same scenario many times before. Just like he had managed before, he would manage again, even if it meant beginning the job hunt yet again.

Not Moshe.

He could not see himself looking for a job again on Monday. Instead of walking home with a sense of pride that he was still able to keep Shabbos, he came to a different decision. He was going to stick with his job, even if it meant working on Saturday. He did not plan on running from one job to another. Those days were over.

But now he had to break the news to his family. During the Friday-night *seudah,* Moshe was much quieter than usual. His wife asked him repeatedly if he was feeling all right, and he kept insisting he was just fine. However, before going to sleep, he dropped the bombshell. "When shul is over tomorrow, don't wait for me to begin eating. I'm not coming home. I'm davening early and going straight to work."

His wife, who seemed to acknowledge his statement, didn't reply.

The next morning, though Moshe woke up with a heavy heart, his decision had been made. It was time to carry through. However, as soon as he began looking for his clothing, he realized something was wrong. As much as he searched, he couldn't find his shirt. Or his pants. Or his shoes. He ran to his closet. It was completely empty. Someone must have broken into their house and stolen all of his clothing. What other explanation could there be?

He tried to awaken his wife, but she wouldn't budge. Now he became suspicious. His wife was normally a light sleeper. Why was she not waking up?

Aha! There hadn't been a break-in. His wife was the one behind the missing garments! When he confronted her she sat up in bed and admitted to hiding his clothing.

Moshe pleaded, "I can't possibly go to work without my clothing. And I can't stay home either. It's a matter of life and death."

She looked at him with a smirk on her face. "If it's a matter of life and death, then don't allow something petty like clothing to stop you from going. If it's so urgent that you go to work, go in your pajamas and slippers — because you're not getting your clothing back!"

With that one wisecrack, the matter was settled.

He never did go to work on Saturday.

After a long talk with his clever wife, Moshe agreed to continue doing whatever was necessary to keep Shabbos sacred.

Today, over 100 years later, they have many generations of Shabbos-observant descendants to show for it.

What's in Your Suitcase?

As the German Army stormed through the unsuspecting communities of Europe and made their way from town to town, the routine was usually the same. First, the tanks and trucks arrived, always accompanied by vicious, barking German shepherds, which terrorized and intimidated the inhabitants of the villages. Shortly after, the Nazis called all the Jews to the town square, where they falsely assured the populace that though they planned on relocating them, there was no cause for concern; nothing would happen to them. The townspeople were thus instructed to pack their belongings. Each family was allowed a suitcase filled with up to 10 kilograms (about 22 pounds) of "essentials." They had until 5 the next morning to report.

Many of the families were more than a bit naïve and hurriedly filled their suitcases with their definition of "essentials."

A few changes of clothing. One pair of shoes. Perhaps a sweater. Those in the know, however, understood that this was a poor charade and the danger was real — although nobody could imagine the full extent of the horrors that lay ahead — and sewed into the fabric of their coats a different type of "essentials": diamonds, jewels, and other valuables. They figured that a time may come when they would need these possessions, and they would put them to good use.

AVRAHAM, WHO WAS IN HIS LATE TEENS, HEARD THE announcement and began frantically running around the house, looking for ways to smuggle everything and anything of value, including cash and jewels. He was a sharp young man and understood what was about to take place.

Surprisingly, his father's reaction was entirely different. He displayed no panic, only calmness. And then he called over his son and made an unusual request. "Can I please trouble you to iron my shirt?"

Avraham wasn't sure he'd heard correctly. Iron his father's shirt? Now? What for?

"But Papa, shouldn't we be packing our suitcases? Shouldn't we be hiding our valuables? We're up against the clock. We are being taken away to a work camp, and it's very possible we'll never return. This isn't the time for ironing shirts. No one is going to check to make sure your clothing is properly ironed for the journey."

Strangely, though, his father calmly repeated his request. "If you don't mind, can I trouble you to iron my shirt?"

With exceptional reverence and respect for his father, Avraham ignored his instincts, went to the closet, and removed a clean shirt. It wasn't really in need of an ironing, but he began to iron it anyway; his father had asked him to. Even so, he tried to hurry it up. After a few minutes of ironing, he shook it out and presented it to his father. But his father noticed a few wrinkles and asked him if he could please iron it some more.

Now Avraham was even more confused. "Papa, don't you realize what's happening now? We can't wait to act. We must pack our suitcase with our valuables." With insistence and urgency in his voice, Avraham pleaded with his father.

His father was quiet — no response. So Avraham redid the ironing until it was perfect. He handed it to his father, who looked deeply into his son's scared eyes and spoke. "To answer your question, I am very well aware of what is happening. I'm not as naïve as you think. But while everybody else is packing their suitcases with valuables such as diamonds and jewels and money, I'm giving you something worth much, much more. I am enabling you to perform the mitzvah of *kibbud av,* about which the Torah teaches, '*Lemaan yaarichun yamecha*' (*Shemos* 20:12). This will help give you life — more than any sum of money."

The two looked at each other, father and son, while tears gushed forth from their eyes. With his newfound understanding, Avraham thanked his father for the opportunity and privilege. Then he held onto his father and buried his head in his shoulder.

The following morning at 5:00, the townspeople gathered in the town square. The Germans, punctual as ever, were there waiting. The dogs barked and the Nazis shouted their orders, as the Jews were taken to a train station and herded off to a concentration camp.

Their suitcases were confiscated the moment they arrived. Valuables and all.

The entire village was wiped out.

Except for one individual.

Avraham.

Years passed. Avraham married and was blessed with children. And then grandchildren.

As he stood underneath his grandson's chuppah, he told this story.

A lone survivor whose father had provided him with the most valuable treasure of all.

The mitzvah of kibbud av va'eim.

Priceless

SHLOMO COULD NOT HAVE BEEN MORE DELIGHTED WITH the offer. He and his wife Gitti and their young family lived in a frum community in the tristate area. While Shlomo learned in kollel, Gitti, a computer programmer by profession, helped support the family.

Though they very much enjoyed their life there, they didn't fully appreciate a life of Torah and mitzvos until the summer of 2005, when Shlomo was offered the position of scholar-in-residence in a Jewishly populated city on the West Coast. Since he was off from yeshivah in the summer, the timing worked out well for him to enjoy a semi-vacation with his family. Shlomo booked tickets for himself and his family and worked diligently to prepare stimulating *shiurim*. Before long, they were on the plane to their destination.

As soon as they arrived, they retrieved their luggage and went to the rental car counter. Back home, Shlomo drove a seven-year-old Toyota Camry. It got him from place to place, but it was definitely nothing fancy. While he wasn't complaining, he was excited to drive a brand-new Mazda.

After loading up the car with their children and their luggage, Shlomo and Gitti drove out to the neighborhood where they would be hosted for their stay. The weather was absolutely perfect, the scenery breathtaking. They could see the snowcapped mountains in the distance.

Shlomo and Gitti carried their children and their belongings into the rabbi's home, where they would be staying for the next two weeks. Before long, it was time for Minchah. Shlomo clicked the key fob; he wasn't used to keyless entry on his old Camry from the 1990s. And just so he could feel good about it, he clicked it a few more times. Pulling up to the shul in a brand-new Mazda filled Shlomo with a sense of *baalebatishkeit*; he had "arrived." But as soon as he parked in the parking lot — between a pristine Porsche and an antique Jaguar with a mahogany interior — he realized he may have jumped the gun a bit. A humbling moment, to say the least. No, this little Mazda definitely did not make the cut.

Still, Shlomo had come to teach and inspire, so teach and inspire he would.

Over the next two weeks, his family enjoyed a wonderful vacation, while Shlomo connected with many of the congregants. He inspired them with his learning and teaching, and they appreciated all he had to offer. He, Gitti, and their family shared a Shabbos lunch with the community members, an experience enjoyed by all.

Shlomo and Gitti were planning on leaving on Sunday. When Shlomo gave his farewell address that Shabbos, he thanked the community for welcoming him and his family, and praised them for their interest in all his classes. As soon as he finished, Sammy, with whom Shlomo had developed a relationship, went up to him.

"Rabbi, I truly appreciate all the time you gave us. But I want to tell you one thing. One morning recently, as I marveled at the gorgeous snowcapped mountains in the distance, it seemed like heaven was touching the earth. I'm not originally from around these parts, so I decided to take a drive out there and get a closer look. I could only imagine how stunning it would be.

"I drove for about two hours but as I came closer and closer, something funny happened. I began to look at those mountains in a completely different light. They weren't gorgeous at all; they were muddy and ugly. And I suddenly wondered how I ever thought they were beautiful in the first place."

Sammy continued, "Rabbi, I remember the first time you pulled up to our synagogue. I saw the way you eyed my antique Jaguar. It *is* a beautiful car. But our lives are not as glamorous as they appear. The fellow in the front row sits together with two bodyguards because there are people after him in a big way. Two rows behind them sits an individual who has no relationship with his children. Our lives are like the snowcapped mountains; when you look at them up close, they're less than appealing.

"You, on the other hand, are blessed. I've seen the way you and your wife interact and the manner in which you play with your children. Here's my offer. I will deliver my Jaguar to your home on the East Coast if you trade with me and give me one day of your life."

Shlomo didn't know what to say. He had come to teach, but was walking away with an invaluable lesson.

Over a decade and a half has passed since that day. Shlomo and his family still have fond memories of their two-week stay, and Shlomo keeps in touch with Sammy.

And every time they speak, Shlomo thanks Sammy for the lesson that changed the way he looks at life.

Spending Wisely

One day, when the Chofetz Chaim was already elderly, a former *talmid* visited Radin and reintroduced himself to him. "*Shalom aleichem*, Rebbi."

"*Aleichem shalom.* And who are you?"

"I am Yankel Krakover, your *talmid* from 40 years ago."

The Chofetz Chaim asked, "Tell me, how are you learning?"

Yankel proudly responded that he was learning every day.

"And how is your *parnassah*?"

"Rebbi, *halevai* all Yidden would be making a *parnassah* like I am. *Baruch Hashem,* I bring in over 2,000 rubles a month!" (The average individual of those days made 40 rubles a month; Yankel was making 50 times that amount.)

When the Chofetz Chaim asked Yankel how he managed to make so much money, he explained that he bought trees in Russia (where there was an abundance of trees) for 10 rubles apiece, and sold them in Poland (where there was a shortage of lumber) for 200 rubles apiece. "One large shipment gives me enough money for a month." The only issue was how to get the trees over the border without paying taxes. And he had managed to work that out.

Concerned, the Chofetz Chaim asked, "But aren't you worried? Do you know that if you get caught, the authorities will punish you severely? They can shoot you in the head! What are you doing? These people take their tax laws very seriously. How can you so blatantly violate their laws? You're risking your life!"

Yankel calmed his rebbi, "This has been going on for 35 years. When I first started, I stood at the border and met the guard who oversaw the tax collection. I began to talk to him and offered him a few cigarettes. In no time at all, we struck up a conversation and he took a liking to me. One day, I asked him how much he made every month. When he told me he made 40 rubles a month, I asked if he wanted to increase his earnings by 200 rubles a month. Now I had his attention; he asked me what he had to do to make the extra money, and I told him exactly what: Nothing.

"'All you have to do,' I elaborated, 'is not look. Turn a blind eye when my merchandise comes through, and I will pay you 200 rubles a month.' The guard was more than happy to accept the deal. And for the past 35 years, he's done his job to perfection."

Yankel finished telling his story to his rebbi, who asked him to repeat it a few times so he could get all the facts straight. Seeing that the Chofetz Chaim was impressed, Yankel dared to make a request. "Rebbi, please give a *berachah,* not for me, but for the guard at the border. He is getting on in years, and my whole business hinges on him. Please give him a blessing that he should be healthy and be able to continue for a long time." The Chofetz Chaim did as he was asked and blessed the guard with many more healthy years.

Then he asked Yankel to escort him to the yeshivah. He wanted him to be there when he spoke. A short while later, they arrived and the Chofetz Chaim walked up to the *aron kodesh.*

"*Talmidim,*" began the Chofetz Chaim, "I just received a visit from my *talmid,* Yankel, who learned here 40 years ago. Do you know how much money he makes every month? 2,000 rubles! And do you know how he makes that money? There is a guard who stands at the border, who can give anyone who tries to cross illegally a bullet in his head. However, he is willing to accept a bribe every month not to look. Thanks to him, not only does Yankel dodge a bullet every month, but he also makes 2,000 rubles.

"Dear *talmidim*! This is how it works, not only down here on earth but also in *Shamayim.* The *Beis Din shel Maalah* has strict rules. And anyone who doesn't listen will have to suffer the consequences. But just as you can down here, you can also give a bribe in *Shamayim.* And when doing so, you can gain an enormous amount."

The Chofetz Chaim continued, painting a picture of what will happen:

After 120 years, man will stand in judgment; there he will find a scale. On one side of the scale will be his mitzvos and on the other side, his aveiros. At first, his mitzvos will be piled on the scale — all of his tefillos and berachos, Shabbasos and Yamim Tovim; the man's good deeds bein adam la'chaveiro and also bein adam laMakom. But though they may add up, many of the angels created by these mitzvos will be scrawny, weak, meager, dried out. This poor nourishment comes from a good deed performed in a less than admirable or unenthusiastic manner, a tefillah gobbled up or garbled or recited by rote, a kindness done with the wrong intentions.

But then the aveiros will be piled onto the other side of the scale. All the lashon hara, sheker, ona'as devarim, gezel, and missed opportunities will be placed there. Unfortunately, they will be substantial, hefty, energetic, healthy-looking.

All of a sudden, before the man's eyes, a malach will approach the side of the mitzvos holding a bellows, and he will blow into the fragile and anemic mitzvos, breathing life into them, making each feeble, pathetic good deed into a strong, robust one.

The man will wonder: "What's going on over here? Isn't this the World of Truth? How can you pump up my emaciated mitzvos into vigorous actions?"

"You are correct," the angel will reply. "This is most definitely the World of Truth. However, just as one is capable of bribing down on earth, you can do the same thing in Shamayim. And just as one is able to escape death and benefit through those bribes, you can do the same in Heaven. You can escape the harsh judgment and be rewarded through a bribe."

The Chofetz Chaim wrapped up his speech. "So what are the bribes in *Shamayim*? They are made of altruism and mercy. *'Kol hamerachem al habriyos merachamin alav min haShamayim* — Anyone who has compassion on Hashem's creatures will receive compassion from Heaven' " (*Shabbos* 151b).

Now Yankel understood why the Chofetz Chaim had brought him to the *beis midrash*. The *bachurim* had a lesson to learn. And so did he. Yankel thanked his rebbi for the *mussar* and committed to increase his *rachmanus* on others.

A wise way to spend.